For Tucker ♡

March 1998

from Suzanne

FROM SHAKESPEARE TO COWARD

To the memory of my parents, Michael and Iris Sharland,

and to all those who came before

FROM SHAKESPEARE TO COWARD

FROM THE GLOBE TO THE PHOENIX THEATRE

A Guide to Historic Theatrical London and the World Beyond

by Elizabeth Sharland

BARBICAN PRESS

Copyright © Elizabeth Sharland

First published in 1997 by
Barbican Press, c/o Amolibros, 5 Saxon Close, Watchet,
Somerset TA23 0BN

Distributed by Gazelle Book Services Limited,
Falcon House, Queen Square, Lancaster LA1 1RN

The right of Elizabeth Sharland to be identified as the author of the
work has been asserted herein in accordance with the Copyright,
Designs and Patents Act 1988

A CIP catalogue record for this book is available from the British
Library

ISBN 0 9531930 0 4

Typeset by Amolibros, Watchet, Somerset

Printed and bound by T J International, Padstow, England

TABLE OF CONTENTS

ILLUSTRATIONS

1   The Globe Theatre, Southwark
2   The Globe interior — re-opened in 1997
3   The Old Vic Theatre
4   Shakespeare's statue in Southwark Cathedral
5   The George Inn, Southwark
6   Rules Restaurant, Maiden Lane
7   The Ivy Restaurant
8   Noel Coward's blue plaque outside his home
9   The Garrick Club
10 Noel Coward's wine bar in the Phoenix Theatre
11 Theatre Royal, Drury Lane on Catherine Street
12 The Opera Tavern Opposite the Theatre Royal
13 Theatre Museum Covent Garden
14 Julie Andrew's dress from *My Fair Lady* in Theatre Museum
15 The Lyceum Theatre where Sir Henry Irving was actor-manager
16 Garrick in the foyer of Theatre Royal
17 The Green Room Club, 9 Adam St, off the Strand — a famous
    theatrical club with historic paintings and posters, it is a late-night
    drinking spot for actors after the show
18 St Paul's Church, Covent Garden, the setting for the first scene of
    My Fair Lady
19 Half-price ticket booth in Leicester Square
20 Edmund Kean in the foyer of the Theatre Royal
21 St Paul's Churchyard
22 David Garrick's house, 27 Southampton Street
23 National Portrait Gallery
24 Herbert Tree's plaque outside Her Majesty's Theatre
25 Arthur Sullivan (of Gilbert and Sullivan); statue on the
    Embankment behind the Savoy Hotel
26 Dress Circle Shop, 57 Monmouth Street
27 The Savoy Hotel
28 George Bernard Shaw's house, Fitzroy Square
29 St Paul's Church, known as The Actors' Church — some plaques
30 More plaques inside St Paul's
31 Henry Irving's statue next to the National Portrait Gallery
32 Ad Lib Restaurant
33 Charlie Chaplin, Leicester Square

Photograph of the George Inn courtesy of the George Inn

Extracts from the anthology *Love from Shakespeare to Coward* first produced at the Theatre Museum, Covent Garden with Corin Redgrave and Daniel Thorndike - see Chapter Nine, pages 56 - 62

PREFACE

The following chapters do not contain a history of London theatre or the theatres, but rather a guide to historic places where the great actors and actresses lived and worked.

People such as Lord Olivier, Sir Ralph Richardson, Sir John Gielgud, Richard Burton trod the same pavements as Garrick, Kean and Irving before them. Walking around Covent Garden you will see many streets named after the most famous, Betterton, Kemble, Garrick, Macklin. It was Macklin who lived to be the oldest actor on record; he died at the age of 106. The areas with the most colourful history are certainly Covent Garden, Leicester Square and The Strand. Garrick lived at 27 Southampton Street, Bernard Shaw lived on Adelphi Terrace, just off The Strand and Irving was working at the Lyceum Theatre, just around the corner.

You probably won't see the famous ghosts but you can walk down the alleyway beside the Adelphi theatre where William Terris, the actor, was murdered outside the stage door, or see, in St Leonard's Church in Shoreditch, the memorial to the two actors who saved Shakespeare's plays from extinction — they were John Hemming and Henry Condell. Or see a statue of Shakespeare as well as of Charlie Chaplin in Leicester Square or the Noel Coward wine bar in the Phoenix Theatre in Charing Cross Road.

Waterloo Bridge could be named London's theatre bridge of the past century because of the journey to the Old Vic Theatre. Generations of famous actors have all made their way there, and now they go to the South Bank as well.

Although the Royal National Theatre could not be classed as an old historic building, the four artistic directors who have run it since it opened will surely be found in the pages of theatre history books — Lord Olivier, Sir Peter Hall, Sir Richard Eyre and Trevor Nunn. So will the Dames! — Sybil Thorndike, Maggie Smith, Judi Dench and Dianna Rigg.

The last great actor-managers also haunt the area. Forbes-Robertson, Herbert Tree, Waller, Granville-Barker all probably visited Rules' Restaurant at one time or another, followed years later by Graham Greene, Clark Gable and John Barrymore. Lily Langtry and the Prince of Wales dined in a private dining room which can still be visited today.

Actors are taught to observe people, to show compassion, to try to delve into other people's souls. In an ideal world they then can demonstrate this on stage, creating characters, continuing to observe, to be curious as they draw upon their knowledge and use it. Because they are, and must be, totally focused on the work at hand, they live in their own world. However, even when there is a break in this routine, they are still observing, their talents resting. What do actors do when they are not working? Well, that is the subject for another book, but the second half of this book is about survival. Travel in my case. This was triggered by the deadly icy English winters.

An actor's curiosity together with the desire to discover another world — almost like Michael Palin — propelled me to focus for a time on distant lands, and to tread in others' footsteps.

INTRODUCTION

FROM TASMANIA TO LONDON

What is the connection, you may ask, between the Theatre Royal in Hobart, Tasmania and the Old Vic Theatre in London?

It's a rhetorical question in a way, like asking Hobart tennis-players, such as the local school champions, why they dream of going to, or better still, playing at Wimbledon. The dreams come from the first stirrings of emotion, admiration and finally ambition. We remember the people and places that first inspired us, the local opera company's production, Joan Sutherland perhaps, or a visiting company at the Theatre Royal.

The Theatre Royal in Hobart is an architectural and historical gem. It was built over a hundred years ago and is almost a replica of the Theatre Royal in Bristol. Laurence Olivier played there in the 1940s and was astonished by the design and the acoustics. There has been a stream of famous artists appearing there, and it has so far escaped the bulldozer and progress.

Many of us remember the theatre productions which first caught our imagination. We in Tasmania had little expectation of seeing them on the other side of the world, but we did.

The young women who left Australia to go to England a decade ago were a bit like Snow Whites looking for their Princes. If they could find a rich husband, so much the better, but most of them simply wanted to do the Grand Tour before returning home.

Australians had always felt close emotional links with England. For many generations they considered themselves Englishmen living in Australia, called England "home" and fought for England in the two world wars. The European conflicts which started those wars meant little to them, but any threat to England did. After the Second World War, when England turned to Europe and abandoned the Imperial Preference system, Australians felt that England was both ungrateful and cold, and began to re-think their traditional loyalties. It must be remembered that they had inherited and embraced not merely English political loyalties and traditions, but English cultural aspirations as well, including British tastes in theatre, nineteenth century opera, music and ballet. And they had once been, like the British, intensely chauvinistic, with a feeling of superiority vis-à-vis the Asian nations. Now they had to face up to the fact that they were now an Asian nation themselves, and that much of their tradition was being swept away.

During our morning assembly at St Michael's Collegiate School we listened to guest speakers who reminded us of our heritage but tried also to broaden our horizons.

Hobart is the gem of Australia. It has the quiet atmosphere of an old whaling town, and the Georgian architecture makes it a very English kind of city. Mount Wellington looms behind the city with a terrific majesty, and the view from the summit is spectacular. No visit to Hobart would be complete if the ride up Mount Wellington were omitted. From there, you can see almost half the island on a clear day, and all the miles of sandy beaches, rivers, inlets, and the Derwent River winding out to sea. Next stop is Antarctica!

Stones of a Century, a book my father wrote in the '50s, was a popular best-seller because it was the first pictorial history of the beautiful Georgian-style architecture in Tasmania, from office buildings to the residences of the Governor General and of rich farmers.

My father was a writer/photographer and he saw the early buildings as something to be restored and treasured. He organised the restoration and opening of Entally, the first home to be placed on the tourist map as a tourist attraction. There is a plaque in the small chapel outside the house in his memory. He also was the only Australian journalist who had a weekly newspaper column for over sixty years, including during the war.

The mountain serves as the chief weather indicator as well. It vanishes in the winter several times a day, enveloped in snow or fog and cloud. The summer is the time to explore it, taking the zigzag path past the rock formation called the Organ Pipes and then visiting the small wood huts along the way for a picnic or sleep over. No Hobart school boy or girl has missed being taken on a hike up the mountain. You are born under its shadow, and when you leave to go abroad, you miss it. In fact Peter Conrad, another Hobartian, wrote a whole book about it.

My hobby of painting landscapes started in London. I began painting scenes from memory. I started work on four canvases featuring the mountain, but I keep going back to it, like Cezanne (*I wish!*) and his fascination with Mont St Victoire which he painted so relentlessly. I haven't got it out of my system yet.

There are a few interesting houses dating from the last century; my Sharland fore-father arrived in Hobart as the first Surveyor-General, built the second house in the city for himself, the first being the Governor-General's, and he went on to explore the island, naming in the process at least one mountain after himself. He also was one the founders of the

Tasmanian Club, to which I cannot go unless invited by a male friend or relative, because women are not eligible for membership. The house I grew up in, Melrose, was not however built by him, being of somewhat later date. It now houses the Tasmanian Ministry of Health.

The Theatre Royal was my focus in those days and my first acting roles were on-stage there in the local repertory company.

Just around the corner is the old City Hall where visiting musicians were performing with our local orchestra.

There was a group of us madly keen on anything and anybody who was visiting from the mainland or better still from overseas.

Arriving in London for the first time from Australia proved unexpectedly stressful. Even now, the British still feel a certain fondness for the colonials, but feel superior to them especially socially, and the overall sentiment towards the new arrivals from Australia was, and still is, tinged with patronising amusement. You quickly learn to get rid of your accent as it marks you as a colonial. Once you have digested this initial shock, you must dismiss it and accept it as part of the experience of living in Britain and forget about it.

During my first two years in London I studied music (piano) and drama at the Guildhall School. Usually you are a music or a drama student, not both. I couldn't decide what I wanted to take up as a career. I sat for my piano exams as well as the drama certificate. So life was rather schizophrenic, with mornings devoted to piano practice and lessons, and the rest of the day studying voice, acting techniques and attending rehearsals at night.

After the Guildhall I went to Felixstowe. It was the coldest winter in twenty years. The theatre was not heated and we all had chilblains and colds most of the time.

During my time at the Guildhall, for extra money I worked front of house at the Old Vic — a few years earlier than Simon Callow had, and like him no doubt, I applied for every audition session they had at the Old Vic.

Finally, a letter arrived in Felixstowe asking me to audition for the Old Vic tour to Australia which was to be led by Robert Helpmann and Katharine Hepburn. A few weeks later, another letter arrived; I had been chosen to go on the tour. It was a great moment to phone home and tell them I was coming back — the only Aussie in the company apart from Helpmann.

The only disappointment was that the tour would visit every state, except Tasmania.

CHAPTER ONE

SHAKESPEARE AT THE GLOBE

In June 1997 the new Globe Theatre opened on the South Bank. The American actor and director, Sam Wanamaker, spent over twenty years working on his dream of rebuilding and re-opening Shakespeare's Globe Theatre. Unfortunately he died before the theatre was completed. He battled for money and for support with enormous enthusiasm for his project. One man's achievement made history on the international theatre scene. His vision has now come to fruition and the Globe Theatre will become a focus for playgoers who want to see Shakespeare as it was presented in Shakespeare's day. Much has been written about the new Globe Theatre, and Barry Day's book, *This Wooden "O"*, is the definitive work on the story of the rebuilding. Mark Rylance is now the new Globe's artistic director.

In Shakespeare's time all performances were given during the day for obvious reasons; no electric light was available. Many of the performances were interrupted by hecklers and drunken spectators. Nowadays the interruptions are ones that were not a problem in his era. Jet aircraft and helicopters are the main nuisances and they totally destroy the illusion of an Elizabethan age. The actors have to be congratulated on being able to carry a scene when this happens.

Laurence Olivier's film, *Henry the Fifth*, begins in a film studio's version of the old Globe and it is interesting to note that his son Richard Olivier is now directing the same play at the Globe with Michael Rylance playing Henry. The prologue of the play was performed by Zoë Wanamaker at the Globe last June for the re-opening celebrations.

Of the life of Shakespeare himself we know little with certainty; that he was born in Stratford-on-Avon, that he married Anne Hathaway and had three children, wrote some plays, died while still relatively young, and was buried in his native place, these facts are indisputable; most of the rest is conjecture. The reasons for this obscurity are numerous; in his time actors and playwrights were not as well regarded as they subsequently became, and indeed, after his death, the Puritan revolution succeeded in abolishing theatre completely for a time. With the Restoration, theatre was revived, but not his popularity, which did not come into the ascendant again until the nineteenth century.

It is however generally believed that he was born on the 23rd of April, 1564. He was one of eight children, one other of whom also became an actor but died at the age of twenty-eight. He seems to have attended school until he was about fourteen. He married when he was eighteen, his wife being eight years older. He left for London apparently to avoid prosecution for poaching, probably in his early twenties. In London he immediately found work as an actor, and may well have already been one in Stratford. He joined the company playing at the Globe theatre and subsequently at the Blackfriars theatre as well, and all his dramatic works were first produced at one or the other of these two theatres.

His plays attracted attention very quickly, and it was not long before he had become a friend of Ben Johnson; this friendship lasted for the rest of Shakespeare's life. His most useful patrons included the earls of Southampton, of Pembroke and of Montgomery; less useful was the patronage of Queen Elizabeth the First and of King James the First, from both of whom he derived little but honour — the queen being disinclined to spend money on whatever did not have a political purpose, and the king being generally too short of money to help, although both apparently had a sincere appreciation of his genius. It was King James who granted Shakespeare his Royal patent, which had the practical effect of elevating him and his company from being servants of the Lord Chamberlain to being in the employment of the Crown.

He seems to have continued his acting career for at least twenty years, and to have retired a relatively rich man by the standards of his time. He died on his fifty-second birthday in Stratford, having been attended in his last illness by one of his sons-in-law, Dr Hall. The cause of his death is not known.

His only son, Hamnet, had died at the age of twelve; both his daughters married and had children and grandchildren. However no lineal descendants remain.

The first Globe theatre dates from 1599, virtually four hundred years prior to the present structure. The story of its origin is an example of the tenacity and imagination that seems to be necessary for keeping theatre alive in almost any era.

Burbage, the great sixteenth-century actor and supreme Shakespearean exponent had had a theatre built in 1576, which was simply called "The Theatre". It was built on a site owned by a certain Giles Allen, who leased it to Burbage. Burbage died in 1597; his two sons inherited the theatre, but not the site on which it was standing. The lease came up for renewal at the end of 1598; the two Burbage sons expected that the lease would be renewed, but Allen refused to do so. What happened next is more a legend than a definite historical fact, but may be true.

Shortly after Christmas, Burbage and his men disassembled The Theatre, moved the timbers that had composed it across the river to a new site, and the following year, using the timbers of the old theatre, the Globe was built, opening within a few months. Shakespeare continued to act, and write plays, for the new theatre.

However the Globe theatre burnt down, apparently from a spark landing on its thatched roof, in 1613; it was immediately re-built and re-opened the following year, but Shakespeare wrote no more plays, retiring to Stratford-on-Avon, where he died in 1616. The Globe seemed fated; it was deliberately destroyed in 1644 in the general Puritanical campaign against all forms of vice, particularly those inherent in the theatre and ascribed to all who acted in them or who attended. When the monarchy was restored in 1660, although theatre revived, the Globe was not, and the world had to wait for Sam Wanamaker before a new, resplendent Globe Theatre stood proudly once more on the banks of the Thames.

One of the mysteries, among many, about Shakespeare is his knowledge of Europe. Did he travel? Did he know Verona, Venice and Rome? Why was *The Merchant of Venice* set in Venice, and did he have a great love of Italy? Did the freezing weather drive him to warmer climes? One wonders, if he did go, how could he spare the time? Did he need to travel in order to write or did he write purely from his imagination? The plays invoke the period, the atmosphere, and the local colour of these places he was writing about. The thought occurred to me that perhaps he was a peripatetic soul who sought material everywhere, but it was at the Globe Theatre that he captured the magic of these far-flung places.

A Sonnet upon the Pitiful Burning of the Globe Playhouse in London

A Broadsheet Ballad

Now sit thee down, Melpomene,
Wrapped in a sea-coal robe,
And tell the doleful tragedy
That late was played at Globe;
For no man that can sing and say
Was scared on St Peter's Day.
Oh sorrow, pitiful sorrow, and yet all this is true.

All you that please to understand,
Come listen to my story;
To see Death with his raking brand
'Mongst such an auditory;
Regarding neither Cardinal's might,
Nor yet the rugged face of Henry the Eighth.
Oh sorrow, pitiful sorrow, and yet all this is true.

No shower his rain did there down force,
In all that sunshine weather,
To save that great renowned house,
Nor thou, O ale-house, neither.
Had it begun below, *sans doute*,
Their wives for fear had pissed it out.
Oh sorrow, pitiful sorrow, and yet all this is true.

This fearful fire began above,
A wonder strange and true,
And to the stage-house did remove,
As round as tailor's clew;
And burnt down both beam and snag,
And did not spare the silken flag.
Oh sorrow, pitiful sorrow, and yet all this is true.

anon (1613)

4

CHAPTER TWO

THE OLD VIC

Sir Peter Hall revitalised the Old Vic, opening his new repertory company in the 1996-97 season, three years before the millennium. The old theatre has never looked so good. When the Canadian entrepreneur, Ed Mirvish, bought the theatre in the '80s he rented it out to visiting companies, but now it has come into its own again with all the leading London actors and an all-star cast in every production.

When I first worked there as a student, Michael Benthall was the director who was presenting his five-year plan of producing all Shakespeare's plays within that time and inviting guest directors to join him. This was before the National Theatre had been built so all the focus was on his work at the Vic. Laurence Olivier, John Gielgud and Ralph Richardson had all preceded him and Benthall was to discover the fresh new talent that would follow in their footsteps.

He cast a young Richard Burton as Hamlet, Claire Bloom as Ophelia and Michael Hordern as Polonius. It was the training ground for the stars of today. Guest director Franco Zeffirelli cast Judi Dench as Juliet and started her illustrious career.

Every drama student wanted to audition there. One day towards the end of my course at the Guildhall I managed to obtain work on the front of house staff. This meant I could watch the performances. My job after collecting tickets was to remain in the theatre to keep an eye on the audience, to remove their tea-trays from the open thrust of the stage, to remove coats slung over the dress circle and the balcony, and to stop school children from constantly flipping open the metal opera-glass holders noisily during the performance.

I watched Burton's *Hamlet* over fifty times and can still remember every move he made and every inflection in his soliloquies, and also his remarkable stage fight with Robert Hardy as Laertes at the end of the play, which was always played to audiences so hushed you could hear a pin drop as they faced each other, swords in hand.

The audience was enthralled with the magic. It was great theatre and each night I would walk home over Waterloo Bridge, my feet treading on air.

The front of house staff were allowed to eat in the canteen backstage during the matinee and evening performances so we had the opportunity to actually talk to members of the company. I viewed them with awe as if they were almost superhuman: "There is William Squire sitting in the corner; and here comes John Neville." We didn't speak unless we were spoken to. We were allowed to attend the Christmas parties and one evening, in a Paul Jones, I danced with Burton who was not quite sober.

Emma Cons was the woman who founded the Vic and her work was carried on by Lillian Baylis, one of the many deeply inspired individuals who were successful in their endeavours against so many obstacles in keeping the artistic spirit alive. We are so fortunate to have such legacies left by such pioneers. That's what makes the theatre scene so historic and exciting in London. Their monuments are still here — Henry Irving's Lyceum Theatre, Sheridan's Drury Lane, Lillian Baylis at the Old Vic and now of course the new Globe Theatre. People who visit London and miss all this, miss the central core of theatrical and artistic London.

If you think of all the unsigned contracts and choices offered to go elsewhere that are dished out to the leading actors and actresses, you would quickly realise how much they are focused on carrying on a tradition that is legendary. We lose a few to Hollywood, (Richard Burton in the fifties and now Anthony Hopkins) but the others are not so easily seduced.

The Old Vic Theatre was originally built in 1818 and was named the Royal Coburg after one of the donors, Prince Leopold. Unfortunately the theatre was located in a bad area and it became the home of melodramas and crude music hall shows. By 1880 it had just closed and then Emma Cons, a social reformer bought it and redecorated it.

She began by forbidding alcohol, renaming it The Royal Victoria Coffee House, and starting a completely new policy of presenting concerts, musical evenings with extracts from opera, and temperance meetings. To make ends meet, she also opened a college in the rear of the theatre called Morley College. As the work increased, she asked her niece Lilian Baylis, who was a music teacher in South Africa to join her as her assistant.

When Emma Cons died in 1912, Lilian Baylis took over the theatre. She immediately applied for and obtained a licence to produce operas and plays, and two years later she had formed her own drama and opera company. Because there was so little space in the building for dressing rooms, rehearsal and backstage areas, she moved Morley College out in 1923 and gave herself more of a free hand for opera and play productions. She was a religious woman, usually going to mass in the morning on her way to the theatre. It is said that she would often pray: "Please God, send me a good actor, but send him cheap."

She would cook her meals on a gas ring, beside the stage, so quite often the smell of fried sausages drifted across the stage during rehearsals.

Ben Greet became her first resident director for drama and the opera company was run by Clive Barrey and Edward Dent who translated every opera into English. A financial crisis arose and Charles Dance, the impresario, donated £30,000 — so that in the 1923-1924 season the Vic staged twenty operas and eighteen plays, most of them by Shakespeare.

In the 1920s she helped purchase the old Sadler's Wells Theatre in Islington, where more opera could be heard at reasonable prices, and helped Ninette de Valois to start her ballet company which eventually became the Royal Ballet. Her energy and planning was astonishing. She hired directors, actors and set designers. Thus began her illustrious career which helped so much to bring us such talented performers as Sybil Thorndike, Edith Evans, Peggy Ashcroft, Michael Redgrave, Alec Guiness, Laurence Olivier, John Gielgud, not forgetting directors such as Tyrone Guthrie.

Lilian Baylis died in 1937, but not before laying down the idea for a National Theatre. The theatre continued until 1941 — when it was bombed. The company decamped to the New Theatre until the Old Vic re-opened in 1950.

The new National Theatre was established in 1963 at the Old Vic under the direction of Laurence Olivier, and in 1976 the National moved to its present home on the South Bank. Lilian Baylis did more single-handedly for the British theatre than any other woman in history.

CHAPTER THREE

A WALK THROUGH COVENT GARDEN AND SOHO

The portico of St Paul's Church, Covent Garden

Covent Garden is one of the most attractive and popular areas of central London. It is also one of the richest in terms of number and type of theatres and theatre related buildings. A good place to start a walk through this area is the portico of St Paul's, known as the actors' church.

The portico faces onto Covent Garden market — the central focus of the area, and the reason for its existence. This was originally a convent garden — the name was gradually altered by generations of Londoners — that provided fresh vegetables for the monks of Westminster Abbey. Although the monks disappeared with Henry VIII's dissolution of the monasteries in the 1530s, the market remained as a source of food for Londoners, more recently providing vegetables for the smart hotels and restaurants of the West End.

The area used to be owned by the Dukes of Bedford whose coat of arms can still be seen on the outside of the market buildings, the latter having now been converted into shops and wine bars. it was a Duke of Bedford who asked Inigo Jones, an architect but also a theatrical producer of sorts (he organised court entertainments, called masques), to build him a church. He specifically wanted a plain church — "a barn of a place, Jones," — and Inigo Jones was as good as his word, providing what he claimed to be the finest barn in Christendom!

The portico of the church is what interests us at this point, for we shall enter the inside of Inigo Jones' barn at the end of the tour. The portico is imposing without being ornate, and serves as a perfect backdrop for the street entertainers who are such a feature of today's Covent Garden, and whose ancestors, acting out mystery plays and religious stories, were the founders of modern European drama.

The portico has been used to famous effect as the setting for *My Fair Lady*, one of the longest running shows at the Theatre Royal, Drury Lane, and, subsequently, a highly successful film starring Rex Harrison (reprising his stage performance) and Audrey Hepburn. It is in front of St Paul's portico that Stanley Holloway, due to be married in the morning, sings his famous request to "get me to the church on time".

Some three centuries before the film, the same portico was the scene of the first ever Punch and Judy show seen in England. The performance was recorded by no less a personage than Samuel Pepys, probably the most famous diarist in history, whose vivid evocations of Restoration London include many accounts of trips to the theatre, together with appreciative remarks on the charms of Nell Gwynn. An inscription (which makes a change from the inevitable blue plaque!) on the church wall records that Pepys saw the puppet show in 1662, and this was commemorated by the Society for Theatre Research and the British Puppet and Model Guild in 1962. There is still a regular Punch and Judy show in the market, but these days it is on the other side of the market. Despite the passage of three hundred years, the happy absorption on the faces of the watching children, and the nostalgic pleasure of their parents, is the same today as it has ever been.

Leaving the portico behind, walk past the appropriately named Punch and Judy pub, through the covered market, to Russell Street. Just before you reach each, look down into the basement courtyard of the Crusting Pipe, the quaintly named wine bar (part of the prestigious Davys group). In the courtyard, seated at the many tables, with a cold glass of white wine, visitors enjoy live music and opera from music students and professional musicians who are continuing Covent Garden's centuries-old traditions of street theatre.

On the left, as you walk down Russell Street, the Royal Opera House has torn down some attractive eighteenth century coffee houses, in order to extend the Opera House and to re-create Inigo Jones' original plans for the area. This has been a highly controversial project, and only time will tell whether this has been an act of vandalism or an enlightened improvement. On the right, opposite the new buildings, is the Theatre Museum.

The Theatre Museum, Russell Street

The Theatre Museum, an offshoot of the Victoria and Albert Museum in South Kensington, is devoted to the study of the performing arts, so it takes in ballet and opera as well as theatre. Beyond the foyer is an exhibition area with changing themes — a recent one explained the background behind the Royal Opera House's development plans.

Downstairs, past walls covered with the palm prints and autographs of theatrical celebrities, are changing exhibitions and displays of British theatre history, from Shakespearean times to the present day. Make-up demonstrations are a particularly popular attraction, especially for children. The Paintings Gallery is an attractive performance and display area where lectures, recitals, book launches and society meetings are held. The studio theatre was once used for theatre performances, but nowadays it tends to be the provider of interactive workshops (as on theatre costume down the ages). It was the setting for the inaugural meeting of the Irving Society, a new group formed to promote interest in, and knowledge of the life and work of, the greatest Victorian actor-manager, Sir Henry Irving (see Lyceum Theatre).

Scholars have access to the Theatre Museum's superb archive collection of memorabilia and information on past and present actors and productions. This takes the form of press cuttings, books, play scripts, memoirs, photographs and programmes, but has moved with the times in that there is now a video collection as well. The principle behind this innovative idea is that although theatre, by its very nature depends on live performance and the interaction between audience and actors, video recordings of live productions do at least give future generations an opportunity to see actors in action — even if that is, by necessity, a poor shadow of actually being there in the stalls!

Leaving the Theatre Museum, and emerging again into the daylight, turn right and cross the road. Immediately ahead is a huge sign, at the corner of a vast theatre, advertising *Miss Saigon*. This is the Theatre Royal, Drury Lane.

The Theatre Royal, Drury Lane

Known in the business as "The Lane", this is the oldest theatre in London (with all due respect to the reconstructed Globe — see the chapter on The Globe and Shakespeare). As if designed to confuse tourists, the Theatre Royal's entrance is not actually sited on Drury Lane (which runs past the back of the building) but on the less well-recognised (but far more attractive) Catherine Street.

There have been several buildings on the site, a fact explained partly by successive managements' need to increase the size and facilities of the building, and partly because of that perennial London problem in previous centuries — fire.

The Theatre Royal was established by the granting of a Royal Charter by King Charles II, and this charter, the pride of the theatre, used to be displayed on the cover of every Drury Lane programme, until modern marketing and design did away with it. An understandable change, but an unfortunate loss.

After Charles' father, Charles I, had been beheaded by Oliver

Cromwell's regime in 1649, the monarchy had been abolished and with it went the theatre, which was seen as an ungodly and licentious entertainment. When the monarchy was restored with Charles II's return from exile in 1660 (hence the Restoration period of history, usually applied to the years up to his death in 1685), the theatre was restored too.

Despite the King's love of the stage, permission to perform was strictly prohibited, except by licence, given that plays could easily be used for anti-government propaganda. After all, it was following a performance of Shakespeare's Richard II, a play about the deposition of a King, that the Earl of Essex led his ill-fated rebellion against the ageing Queen Elizabeth. The granting of the King's licence was, therefore, vital to respectability and official approval. For many years only two theatres enjoyed this — the Theatre Royal, Drury Lane, and the Theatre Royal, Haymarket (see the chapter on West End theatres) hence their names.

The Theatre Royal saw many visits from King Charles, though he was attracted not so much by the plays as by the female players — another change that he had brought about, for earlier in the century, during his father and grandfather's reigns, female parts had been played by teenage boys.

Charles had many mistresses but the most famous, and certainly the most popular, was Nell Gwynn, an actress at Drury Lane. She had started her theatre career as an orange seller, which was something of a cross between an usherette and a prostitute. Graduating to the stage, she demonstrated a talent as a light comedienne, and caught the King's eye, and later his heart.

One could write a book on Nell Gwynn alone, but we must move on, leaving her to her place in history, along with all the other ghosts of past performers. Many theatres have a resident ghost, and Drury Lane has a mysterious figure in eighteenth century clothes. Workmen digging away at a wall as part of a refurbishment project found the skeleton of a man, dating from this period, with a dagger in his ribs, so perhaps the ghost story is well founded! The theatre, now owned by Stoll Moss, the largest theatre chain in the West End, organises frequent tours (details from the box office), in which this and many other stories and anecdotes relating to the theatre can be heard.

Of the cast of actors and actresses who have appeared at The Lane, a few should be mentioned. David Garrick, one of the most famous actors ever, who brought to the profession a great talent and a much needed professionalism, ran the theatre with a showman's eye and a businessman's brains, employing all the greatest actors of the age — particularly the formidable Mrs Siddons. She was an actress of forbidding appearance and a superb tragedienne, particularly in the role of Lady Macbeth. When Sheridan, the brilliant young playwright whose work Garrick put on at Drury Lane, and who took over the ownership of the theatre from him, was asked whether he had ever considered an affair with her, he replied that he would as soon have an affair with the Archbishop of Canterbury!

Sheridan wrote comedies that were quickly recognised as classics: *The Rivals, The Critic,* and *The School For Scandal.* Yet despite his success as a playwright, his greatest ambition was to be a politician, and he used his considerable income from the stage in furtherance of a political career, most of which was spent on the opposition benches.

Sheridan was a far better playwright than he was a theatre manager. He spent a fortune on refurbishing the Theatre Royal, only to have it burn down in a catastrophic fire in 1809. The news of the disaster was brought to him during a debate in the House of Commons, but he displayed a typically British stiff upper lip, refusing to have the business of the House interrupted by a personal misfortune. Only after he had finished his contribution to the debate did he feel free to attend to the theatre.

Fire-fighting in those days was more or less limited to stopping the flames reaching adjacent buildings, so there was nothing that could be done to save the theatre. Ironically, Sheridan had had a huge water tank created for just such an emergency, but it had been drained for routine maintenance at the time that the fire took hold — a typical example of the bad luck that was to dog his time as a theatre owner. As if that were not bad enough, he was not insured!

Even at this moment of crisis, however, Sheridan's famous wit did not desert him. His friends, searching for him amid the confusion and crashing timbers, the flames and the dense smoke, found him at a nearby inn. When asked how he could bear to watch his fortune and his livelihood literally going up in smoke, he simply smiled and asked them, "May a man not take a drink at his own fireside?"

Although the theatre was, of course, rebuilt, Sheridan was a broken man. His political career fared no better, and he even fell out with the Prince of Wales who, on his father George III being declared insane, was made Prince Regent (1810). There had never been any love lost between George III and his heir; indeed his legendary dislike of his eldest son accounts for the extraordinary fact of there being two royal boxes at Drury Lane.

The incident that sparked this was that when the King came across the Prince of Wales in the foyer of the theatre, in a fit of rage he physically attacked him! The King was eventually restrained, but it was decided that, in order to prevent such an unseemly event occurring again, there should be two royal boxes, each with their own staircase — hence the King's Side and the Prince's Side today. Once in their boxes, though they could not avoid seeing each other, they were at least prevented form coming to blows.

There was nothing to stop other people from having a go at them, however. Boxes were designed for the occupants to be seen, rather than for them to see the stage, which is why the sight lines from them are generally bad (in all theatres), and why today's Royals (especially Princess Margaret) often prefer to be seated in the middle of the Dress Circle, rather than in a box.

George III was on one such visit to Drury Lane, accompanied by Sheridan, when a madman attempted to assassinate him with a pistol shot. Fortunately his aim was as poor as his reasoning, and the King was able to wave to a relieved audience. Sheridan, quick-witted as ever, composed an impromptu extra verse to the National Anthem (about saving the King from assassins) and had the orchestra play it to a delighted King and his enthusiastic subjects.

The Theatre Royal, Drury Lane, saw many great actors during the nineteenth century, a selection of whom are represented by busts in the rotunda on the first floor. The man who has the greatest claim to the title, King of Drury Lane, was, however, a twentieth century theatrical phenomenon, Ivor Novello. Ivor (as he was known to friends, family and fans alike) is described in more detail in the chapter on him (see Ivor Novello's London) but it would be helpful to mention at this point that his string of spectacular musicals saved Drury Lane from closure in the mid 1930s, and ensured its survival for the rest of that decade.

Beginning with *Glamorous Night* in 1935, and continuing with *Careless Rapture* (1936) and *Crest of The Wave* (1937), then finishing with *The Dancing Years* (1939) he effortlessly wrote, composed and then starred in his own musicals. They owed a great deal to those of Frank Lehar, but they all demonstrate a style that is very much Novello's own. In the year "off", 1938, he decided to ring the changes by playing in, of all things, Shakespeare and, of all plays, *Henry V.* Given his reputation as a handsome matinee idol and composer of lush, romantic music, the role of the young warrior King (Ivor was forty-five at the time) might seem ill-chosen, and the casting of one of his leading ladies, Dorothy Dickson (a Broadway dancer and noted beauty, with whom he had co-starred in *Careless Rapture* and *Crest of The Wave*) as Catherine of France, was unexpected to say the least. A combination of these factors, together with the fact that the Munich crisis took people's minds off the theatre, meant that Ivor's *Henry V* had mixed reviews and a short run.

Musicals have been a feature of Drury Lane ever since. The long run of *My Fair Lady* has already been referred to. *Miss Saigon*, the current production, has hit the record books, and among the shows in between was *Billy*, the musical that helped make the careers of both Michael Crawford and Elaine Page. Despite his later success in *Barnum*, in Andrew Lloyd Webber's *The Phantom of the Opera*, and in his enormously popular *Las Vegas* extravaganza, Michael Crawford is perhaps still best known for his role of Frank Spencer in the 1970s TV sitcom, *Some Mothers Do Have 'Em*.

The best-loved sitcom of them all, *Dad's Army*, also appeared at Drury Lane in the 1970s, and though not as successful in theatrical terms as it had been on the small screen, it has given a great deal of pleasure to its army of fans.

Leaving the splendid foyer of Drury Lane, and saying farewell to over three centuries of the London theatre that it represents, we walk down Catherine Street past the Duchess Theatre.

The Duchess Theatre, Catherine Street

If the Theatre Royal, Drury Lane represents the venerable history of the London Stage, then the Duchess is an example of a jazz age Art Deco theatre from the late 1920s (very late — it opened in November 1929) that has survived the vicissitudes of the twentieth century to become a versatile and much liked performing house for revivals and modern plays alike.

Jessica Tandy scored an early success in *Children in Uniform* in 1932, directed by Leontine Sagan. A rare example (now as well as then) of a woman director, she was later hired by Ivor Novello to direct *Glamorous Night* just up the road at the Theatre Royal.

Playwrights as varied as Emlyn Williams, J B Priestly, William Douglas Home and Harold Pinter have all had successful shows put on here. Although *Oh Calcutta!*, *Run For Your Wife* and *The Dirtiest Show in Town* all appeared at the Duchess, it is best known for the sixteen years that it was home to *No Sex Please, We're British*. The Duchess' refusal to be typecast has been shown by the vast difference between three of her latest shows, *Don't Dress for Dinner* (a farce), Maureen Lipman —*Live and Kidding* — a one-woman revue, and the Royal Shakespeare Company's drama, *The Herbal Bed*.

From the Duchess Theatre, turn right into Exeter Street. A few yards walk will take you to the junction with Wellington Street and, just across the road from you is the imposing facade of the Lyceum Theatre, recently restored at a cost of several million pounds by the Apollo Leisure Group.

The Lyceum Theatre

There has been a theatre on this site since the 1790s, and it was to the Lyceum that the Theatre Royal, Drury Lane turned for a temporary home after the disastrous fire of 1809. Perhaps the actors brought their bad luck with them, for the Lyceum burnt down too, in 1830. This proved an opportunity for greatly increasing the size of the theatre and the splendour of its appearance, and The Lyceum's elegant facade has been a London landmark ever since.

The theatre's claim to fame rests not in its architecture, but in its association with a giant of the theatre world and the first actor ever to be knighted — Sir Henry Irving. Hired in 1871 by the Lyceum's American owner, Colonel Bateman, Irving proved to be an electrifying actor. When, only four years later, Bateman died, Irving took on the management of the theatre as well.

The next two decades saw the Lyceum become the cultural powerhouse of the capital and, thanks to its success, one of the most fashionable places to be seen as well. This was the result of Irving's combination of Victorian melodramas (most notably The Bells) in which he excelled, and a series of lavish Shakespearean productions in which he starred opposite Ellen Terry, one of the most beautiful, as well as gifted actresses of the century. Amazingly, she carried on acting into the era of the silent movies so one can see this star of the 1880s on film, with Ivor Novello and Gladys Cooper, in *The Bohemian Girl* (1922).

Irving's domination of London's theatreland was largely due to his talent on stage, his relationship with Ellen Terry and his ability to spot and employ young actors and actresses of promise, but it was also due to his inspired choice of business manager — a stage-struck Irishman called Bram Stoker. Remembered these days for his novel *Dracula* (1897), Stoker was an indispensable help to Irving, and wrote a highly entertaining and informative book about his time with the great actor-manager.

Among many anecdotes was one describing a visit to the seaside, in search of peace and quiet. An old fisherman agreed to row them both out to sea for a couple of hours relaxation. As they set off, a crowd gathered on the shore, waving frantically. Irving, accustomed to the adulation of the public, waved regally and smiled, acknowledging their applause, while the fisherman carried on rowing out to sea, where a number of Royal Navy warships were to be seen in the distance. Suddenly there was a tremendous explosion as a sheet of water rushed towards the sky. "Oh Lord," said the fisherman, "I forgot. They're testing them new torpedoes today!" The crowds had not been cheering England's finest actor — they had been desperately trying to warn him to get back to shore.

Irving's reign ended in 1902, partly due to old age, partly due to changing public taste, but largely because of the inevitable curse of theatreland — fire. A huge fire destroyed his vast warehouse full of the scenery and costumes that he had accumulated over twenty years, and he could not afford to replace it all.

His leaving was rapidly followed by the demolition of the theatre (though the facade was retained). Shortly before the hallowed walls were pulled down, over a thousand actors gathered in the auditorium for a meeting at which it was decided to ask the government to support the creation of a National Theatre. A historic moment, even if it took many years finally to achieve.

The Lyceum's subsequent history was varied, to say the least. Reopened in 1904 as a music hall, in competition with Oswald Stoll's London Coliseum in St Martin's Lane, the theatre changed hands again six years later, and was then the setting for variety shows, musicals and ballet, Ninette de Valois making her London debut there in 1915.

The Melville brothers, who had run the theatre since 1910, died within a year of each other, in 1937 and 1938, after which the Lyceum was closed as part of a road-widening scheme — the theatre was to be replaced by a roundabout! The last performance before the Lyceum was closed was of *Hamlet*, in which John Gielgud played the lead role. Another great Shakespearean actor, Donald Wolfit, attempted, after the War, to save it as a playhouse, but his gallant efforts failed, and it was converted into a dance hall, then was allowed to rot until Apollo Leisure refurbished and reopened it in 1996, with a production of Andrew Lloyd Webber's *Jesus Christ, Superstar*.

After leaving the Lyceum, walk back up Wellington Street, then turn left into Tavistock Street, which runs behind the Theatre Museum. This takes you into Southampton Street where, almost immediately opposite, stands David Garrick's house, an elegant eighteenth century mansion with a bronze-coloured plaque and bas-relief profile of the great actor, whose association with the Theatre Royal, Drury Lane has already been described.

Dr Samuel Johnson, the compiler of the first English dictionary, was an admirer of Garrick, of whom he said, in a phrase that could as easily have been applied to Henry Irving a century later:, "Here is a man who has advanced the dignity of his profession." His epitaph on hearing of Garrick's death, became famous, and has been applied to many other public figures. "I am disappointed in that death which has eclipsed the gaiety of nations and impoverished the public stock of harmless pleasure."

Having looked up at Garrick's house, carry on straight ahead into Maiden Lane.

Maiden Lane

An attractive old street, this is the site of Rules restaurant (see chapter on London's theatre restaurants) which has been a favourite with actors successful enough to afford the prices, since it first opened in the 1790s. It is the oldest restaurant in London. On the left are the stage door of the Vaudeville and Adelphi theatres. Today's Adelphi stage door is immediately next to what used to be the stage door — the latter has a rather battered-looking Royal coat of arms over it. It was just outside the original stage door that William Terris, a handsome leading man who had learnt his trade under Henry Irving at the Lyceum, met his death; a jealous fellow actor stabbed him to death. It is said that his ghost has been seen in the area.

At the end of Maiden Lane turn right into Bedford Street and head north, until you come to the junction with New Row, Garrick Street and King Street. On the left, some way into Garrick Street, can be seen the Garrick club, a gentlemen's club named after David Garrick. It has many actor members but no actresses, as women are allowed in only as guests. The soot-stained exterior, a relic of Victorian London, hides a splendid interior and a remarkable collection of memorabilia .

Turning right, one enters King Street, an attractive road of eighteenth century houses, smart coffee houses and cafes, and the site of, on the corner with Garrick Street, the world famous clothes shop, Moss Bros. Many an actor has made the pilgrimage to this stately building in order to be properly clothed (morning suit, with black morning coat and grey and black striped trousers, with black top hat) for an investiture at Buckingham Palace, to receive a decoration or, in a few cases, Knighthood or Damehood, for services to the theatre. This transformation is all the more marked these days, when actors and actresses, off stage, look no different to the rest of the public. A far cry from the 1940s and 1950s, when Binkie Beaumont, the doyen of London theatre managers, who dominated the commercial West End, insisted that his stars dress like stars!

St Paul's, Covent Garden

A low, narrow turning on the right of King Street, shortly before reaching the crowded Piazza, leads to the churchyard of St Paul's, an oasis of greenery and flowers in the heart of the city.

If anything, the main body of the church is even simpler than the facade. Although simplicity has its attractions, it can lack character, but St Paul's more than makes up for the lack of architectural detail by the profusion of plaques and commemorative tablets to generations of actors and actresses.

Most of the famous names of British film and theatre can be found here, in the Actors' Church, which is frequently the setting for packed memorial services for the best known members of the profession. Noel Coward, Terence Rattigan, Ivor Novello, Vivien Leigh — all are commemorated here. At the very back of the church the plaques are of wood, and there is a charming tradition of adding to the usual details of name and dates of birth and death, an appropriate quotation from a play (usually Shakespearean) to illustrate the character of the person. Vivien Leigh's, for example refers to death having in his possession "A Lass Unparalleled".

As in books, so on walls, it is often the things that are left out that tell us as much as those that are said. Jessie Matthews was a star in the 1930s. Her slim figure and huge eyes, together with a sweet singing voice and her talent as a dancer (the Americans had wanted her to appear in films with Fred Astaire) had made her the highest paid female performer in the country, both on stage and in a series of British films. Unfortunately she was as headstrong as some of the characters she played. One of her better songs, *Gangway*, summed up her approach to life, which included a ruthless disregard for other people's marriages.

Her seduction of Sonny Hale, the husband of the beautiful and very popular (within the profession as well as among the public) Evelyn Laye, was the last straw, and it was this action that is thought to be the reason that Jessie Matthews, despite her fame, has never had a plaque named after her in St Paul's. More appropriately, perhaps, she has had a bar named after her by one of her greatest fans, Andrew Lloyd Webber, in the nearby Adelphi theatre in the Strand.

It seems appropriate, given that Covent Garden originated with a church garden, that we should have ended the walk, as we began, at St Paul's Church, where Ellen Terry's ashes rest in a silver casket, and where generations of theatre cats are quietly buried in the bushes of the churchyard.

Chapter Four

Places of Theatrical Interest

Shaftesbury Avenue is in the heart of theatreland today. The famous theatres on this street are worth a book of their own. The Lyric, Queen's, the Globe and the Apollo. The Globe is now renamed the Gielgud and it is where the impresario/producer Binkie Beaumont had his office above the theatre overlooking his empire. Richard Hugget's book on Beaumont described in some detail what went on in that office. Further on, there is the Palace Theatre on Cambridge Circus and then Shaftesbury to top them all up, near Holborn. Some of the plays presented at these theatres certainly don't measure up to the quality and elegance of their splendid interiors.

Now, let us visit three other places, which are famous for their own particular brands of drama.

The Royal Opera House

This chapter should include a visit to one of the most famous opera houses in the world, The Royal Opera House in Covent Garden, but as most of the world knows, the theatre is now closed for extensive renovations, and the front entrance has been boarded up and is hidden from view. This whole area of Covent Garden will be in a state of change for a year or so.

Located in Covent Garden, facing the Bow Street Magistrates Court, the present Opera House was built in 1858 as a theatre. The first theatre on this site was built in 1732, and was used primarily for stage plays, although three of Handel's operas had their premieres there in the 1730s. Sheridan's *The Rivals* was first produced there in 1775, and Oliver Goldsmith's *She Stoops to Conquer* in 1773. This theatre burnt down in 1808, and was rebuilt the following year, and saw stage performances by Sarah Siddons, Charles Kemble and Edmund Kean. Fire destroyed this theatre also, in 1856, paving the way for the present structure, the magnificent Royal Opera House, devoted from the beginning to opera, at first in Italian only, (indeed the theatre was called initially the Royal Italian Opera) until 1888, when Augustus Harris took over, and operas were performed in their original languages or in English. The Royal Ballet also made the Royal Opera House its home. Virtually all the most distinguished opera singers and ballet dancers have performed here, including Margot

Fonteyn, Robert Helpmann, Nureyev, Maria Callas, Birgit Nilsson, Kiri Te Kanawa and others — the list is endless. Among conductors, George Solti and Colin Davis have been associated with memorable and repeated triumphs.

The Coliseum

Home of the English National Opera, the Coliseum can be identified by the illuminated globe above the theatre which is visible for miles around. The theatre was built in 1904 by Frank Matcham, an Australian, for the great theatre manager Oswald Stoll, another Australian. The publicity surrounding the opening was enormous and crowds used to attend the variety shows which at the time played four times a day.

After variety shows lost their popularity, the theatre became the home of musical comedy, and the show, *White Horse Inn*, broke all records in the 1930s. Noel Coward, Ivor Novello, Gertie Lawrence, Gracie Fields, Bea Lillie all played there.

The theatre has had a chequered career; it was the home of some of the great American musicals in the 1950s and 1960s, including Ethel Merman in *Call Me Madam*, *Guys And Dolls*, *Damn Yankees*, and *The King and I*.

It is one of London's largest and most elaborate theatres, and it is very much worth your while to attend an operatic performance there.

The Palladium

Situated near Oxford Circus, on the corner of Argyll and Marlborough streets, the Palladium was the real home of "Variety", as it is known in England, or "Vaudeville", in the United States. Its architect was the same Frank Matcham who built the Coliseum, among other theatres. Previous structures on the site included the town house of the Duke of Argyll, a shopping complex and a skating rink. The present building opened in 1910, and almost every form of popular entertainment has found a venue there. Variety shows have featured Gracie Fields and George Robey. It has been the "studio" for television variety shows, pantomime, revues and musicals. American stars have been prominent here since the 1940s, including Frank Sinatra, Ethel Merman, Danny Kaye, Liberace, and later Judy Garland and Liza Minelli, to mention but a few. Apart from individual performances, musicals with large American casts have been produced here including *The King And I*, with Yul Brynner, and *La Cage Aux Folles*.

As well as all the theatres in the West End which are an absolute

1 The Globe Theatre, Southwark (*above*)

2 The Globe interior - re-opened in 1997 (*below left*) **3** The Old Vic Theatre (*below right*)

4 Shakespeare's statue in Southwark Cathedral (*above*) 5 The George Inn, Southwark (*below*)

6 Rules Restaurant, Maiden Lane (*above*) 7 The Ivy Restaurant (*below*)

8 Noel Coward's blue plaque outside his home (*above left*) 9 The Garrick Club (*above right*)

10 Noel Coward's wine bar in the Phoenix Theatre (*below*)

11 Theatre Royal, Drury Lane on Catherine Street (*top right*)

12 The Opera Tavern, opposite the Theatre Royal (*below*)

THEATRE MUSEUM
NATIONAL MUSEUM OF THE PERFORMING ARTS
THEATRE MUSEUM
£3.50
CONCS £2.00

13 The Theatre Museum, Covent Garden (*opposite*)

14 Julie Andrews' dress from *My Fair Lady* in the Theatre Museum (*top right*)

15 The Lyceum Theatre, where Sir Henry Irving was actor-manager (*below*)

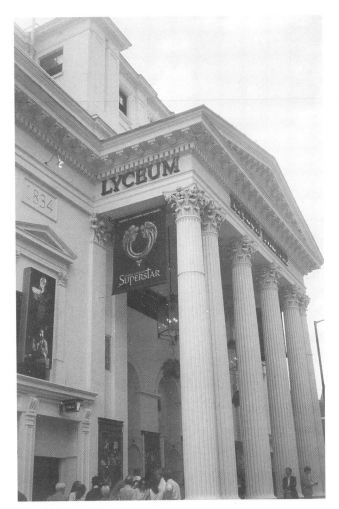

GARRICK

16 Garrick in the foyer of the Theatre Royal (*left*)

17 The Green Room Club, 9 Adam Street, off the Strand - a famous theatrical club with historical paintings and posters, it is a late night drinking spot for actors after the show (*below*)

joy to discover, there are several other places that any theatre lover should visit.

Go to the Strand and down Villiers Street to the Players Club, underneath the arches. Here you will find a Victorian music hall underneath the Charing Cross Railway station. The show there is called *Late Joys* and is, so far as I know, the only theatre that is open on Sunday nights and where you can take your drink with you to your seat. In fact the management encourages it, as there is a toast to The Queen (Queen Victoria) before each performance. It is a memorable little theatre and *The Boyfriend* was first performed here before moving to the West End.

The *Late Joys* programme includes a sing-along of some of the old Victorian music-hall songs such as:-

> I'm a young girl and have just come over
> > Over from the country where they do things big;
> And amongst the boys I've got a lover,
> > And since I've got a lover, why I don't care a fig!
>
> "The boy I love is up in the gallery,
> > The boy I love is looking now at me;
> There he is can't you see? Waving his handkerchief,
> > As merry as a robin that sings on the tree."

If you continue down Villiers Street, around the corner on Northumberland Avenue, you will come to the Playhouse Theatre, where George Bernard Shaw's first play was produced in 1894 — *Arms and The Man*.

Further on, walking to Trafalgar Square, you will find the famous Sherlock Holmes pub with its small museum in a room up on the first floor.

On reaching Trafalgar Square you will find the famous church of St Martins in the Fields. The church and crypt are well worth a visit. This is the church which is most often used for memorial services in eulogy of famous theatre people. The Actors' Church in Covent Garden is also regularly used for this purpose although is often too small. Noel Coward writes that he was asked to speak at Vivien Leigh's memorial service but declined because he thought he might not get through it without breaking down.

The National Portrait Gallery

Located in St Martin's Place beside the National Gallery on Trafalgar Square, the National Portrait Gallery is one of the best-loved institutions in London.

Set up in the 1850s to commemorate Britain's most distinguished citizens, it blends Victorian splendour with twentieth century style, classical symmetry with post-modern design, and the best of portrait painting with glamorous and innovative photography by the likes of Cecil Beaton (who was also a distinguished theatrical designer.)

Although the NPG, (as it is affectionately known by Londoners) has its full share of royalty and generals, admirals and explorers, statesmen and aristocrats, it is also home to a fascinating collection of paintings and photos of the actors and actresses who have made — and retained — London's reputation as the world capital of Theatre.

This, indeed, is reflected in the two statues that flank the National Portrait Gallery. On one side, in St Martin's Place, is a dramatic statue of Nurse Edith Cavell, a British nurse who was shot, found guilty on charges of spying, by the Germans (1915) during the First World War. At the base of the statue are her famous last words, with which, calmly, she faced her end: "Patriotism is not enough; I must have no hatred or bitterness towards anyone." Dame Anna Neagle, one of Britain's most popular actresses from the 1930s to the 1960s, played Edith Cavell in one of her most successful films.

On the other side, in the appropriately named Irving Street, is a statue of Sir Henry Irving, Britain's first actor-knight, and a leading light on the London stage in the last thirty years of the nineteenth century.

Inside the Gallery you will find portraits of actors from all the historical periods represented in the NPG's collection. On the top floor you will find portraits of Vanburgh and Congreve, the playwrights, and paintings of Mrs Siddons, John Philip Kemble, her brother, the great actor-manager, David Garrick, and Edmund Kean, the extraordinary early-nineteenth century artist whose performances were so exciting that a contemporary described watching him on stage as like "reading Shakespeare by lightning".

In the Victorian rooms Irving can, of course, be found, as can his greatest leading lady, Ellen Terry, in a portrait by her husband, G F Watts, which shows the blonde teenager with the exquisite, yet expressive, face smelling the scent of a flower. This is one of the most attractive images on sale in the NPG shop.

Lovers of musical theatre will want to wander from the Terry portrait to the nearby paintings of W S Gilbert and Sir Arthur Sullivan, the most famous double act of the Victorian musical stage, for whose enormously popular shows the Savoy theatre was built. Those with a slightly more operatic taste will be delighted to see Adelina Patti, the leading diva of her day. All three can be enjoyed on the audio guide to the Gallery available from the information desk on the first floor (by the main staircase).

Most of the performers whom visitors will recognise, and will have seen on stage and screen, can be seen in the late twentieth century galleries, also on the first floor.

The Gallery is supposed to represent leading British personalities, But some of the most famous figures in American popular culture (Elizabeth Taylor, Cary Grant, Bob Hope) were born in England, and are, therefore, celebrated on the walls of the NPG.

Miss Taylor, in particular, has pride of place, with a huge Warhol print of her that emphasises her large and sensuous mouth, the red of her lips almost leaping off the walls to plant a smacking kiss on the visitors! The Taylor lips have, recently, become a marketing tool for the NPG, whose stylish shop now sells cuff-links and ties emblazoned with La Taylor's pout.

Beautiful actresses are to be found in a number of rooms, from the surrealist photo of Audrey Hepburn by Angus McBean, to studies of Maggie Smith and Edith Evans, Julie Christie and Julie Andrews, a painting of Peggy Ashcroft, a collection of photos by Dorothy Wilding of glamorous inter-war year actresses like Gladys Cooper, and (by McBean again) stunning camera studies of Vivien Leigh.

Vivien Leigh remains one of Britain's (and America's) most enduring stars, a position that will be guaranteed as long as there is a remaining print of *Gone With The Wind*. The NPG collection has a number of photos of her, as well as some sketches, and, as is appropriate, given that they were theatre's Golden Couple for so many years, several studies of her and her husband, Laurence Olivier.

Despite being an English rose, Vivien's greatest roles were always as American women — Scarlett O'Hara in *Gone With The Wind* and Blanche du Bois (on stage and screen) in *A Streetcar Named Desire*. Divorced from Laurence Olivier, living with her last lover, Jack Merrivale, in fashionable Eaton Square, she died aged only fifty-three (in 1967), leaving behind her a legacy of great acting roles, and the enduring memory of a star — whom everyone who met her invariably refer to as — the most beautiful woman they had ever seen.

Among the male actors there are Dirk Bogarde, the handsome leading man of many British films in the 1950s, and '60s stars like Alan Bates and David Hemmings, to today's leading men, such as Kenneth Branagh and Ralph Fiennes.

The ambivalent love affair between England and America was one of the many subjects of the wit of Oscar Wilde, who has, recently, had a room devoted to sketches and sculptural designs for the proposed new statue to him to be created by Maggi Hambling, a leading modern artist.

Wilde famously declared, on being interrogated by customs officials on his arrival at New York, "I have nothing to declare but my genius." He also said, à propos of the fact that he was preparing to visit the States to give a revenue-raising lecture tour: "Of course, if one could afford to go to America...one would not go!"

This most extraordinary, talented and tragic of men has exerted a fascination for the general public ever since he first burst onto the London literary scene, moving on from there to capture the West End with a string of brilliant plays that reveal not only his wit, but his ability to analyse, and criticise, society. They also, as in *An Ideal Husband*, reveal an understanding of human nature, and a compassion, that were notable for their absence in society's treatment of him at the moment of his greatest trial (in both senses of the word).

Wilde could have escaped his arrest at the Cadogan hotel in Knightsbridge by fleeing the country, as his friends advised him. Indeed, it has been suggested that this is what the authorities wanted too, being afraid of facing the most effective speaker of his day, in the courts. Wilde's own grounding in Greek tragedy (he was a distinguished classics scholar at Oxford) together with his need to be in the London theatre world in order to flourish as a person and earn a living as a playwright, meant that he felt he had little real option but to stay and face his enemies. By an irony that he would have enjoyed, the English actor who plays him in the 1997 film, *Wilde*, is Stephen Fry. Unable to face the lesser trial of hostility from theatre critics, Fry famously disappeared from his lead role in a Simon Gray play at the Albery theatre, and fled on a ferry to Belgium. Fry's painting hangs a few feet away from the current display on Wilde's new statue, and demonstrates the continuity and interaction of the British theatre.

Pausing here before continuing north, you might like to make a detour to view the final resting place of many of these illustrious people by going over to Westminster Abbey and visiting Poets' Corner where writers, poets, actors, artists and politicians are finally united by death.

Although it does not have a Poets' Corner, St Giles-in-the-Fields, located just behind the Phoenix Theatre in St Giles High Street is another historic building with theatre connections. Founded as a leper hospital by Matilda, Queen of Henry 1st in 1101, the chapel survived until the present church was built in 1734. The beautiful Palladian interior houses an organ from 1671 and Wesley's pulpit from the West End chapel. Parish registers dating from 1561 contain hundreds of historic names including those of Cibber, Kemble, Garrick, Hansard, Shelley and Byron. The memorial service for John Osborne, the playwright, was held here.

From Trafalgar Square walk up St Martin's Lane to Cecil Court. In this court is a row of bookshops which are unique — ballet books, travel books, posters, collectors' items; and best of all is David Drummond's bookshop specialising in theatre. He has a marvellous collection of memorabilia and posters.

Continuing up St Martin's Lane you come up to Monmouth Street eventually and on your right is another "must", the Dress Circle Theatre Shop; here you can find CDs, tapes and videos of dozens of West End and Broadway shows. It is the meeting place for many performers, and you may spot a celebrity having a coffee at nearby cafe.

Just around the corner on Tower Street is the Actors' Centre. This was first opened by Laurence Olivier as a place for professional actors to have their own club, take workshops and have private coaching. The small theatre there, the Tristan Bates theatre, is named after Alan Bates' son who died tragically young, a few years ago. Although the Actors' Centre is a private club for actors, the theatre performances are open to the public and it is worth while picking up a programme of what's on, as you may see a new play or a new star that evening. There is a bar in the basement, also open to the public.

Moving on to Cambridge Circus, you are now right opposite Soho. Walk along Old Compton Street and you see the old Coach and Horses pub on the corner of Greek Street, which the writer/wit/raconteur Jeffrey Bernard made famous. Next on the left in Dean Street is the French Pub which is worth a visit. Look at the old photos and newspaper clippings on the walls. This was the headquarters for the Free French during the war, and the then proprietor, Gaston, became famous as the leader of the movement and sheltered many Frenchmen during that period. It is also frequented by theatre people especially at lunch time. Many of the regulars are well known and are usually delighted to chat.

Then to Kettners — once a fancy restaurant but now serving mostly pizzas; it has a famous past and was where all the young hopefuls who were trying to get into the movies went for a drink. Wardour Street, the film production centre, is nearby. Dirk Bogarde, Sean Connery, Stewart Granger and many others dined here. You could go back down to Shaftesbury Avenue. The restaurants associated with theatre in Soho include The Gay Hussar on Frith Street, and, last but not least, Quo Vadis, where many a movie deal was made.

There are dozens of eating places from the cheap Stock Pot menus, to L'Escargot and Conran's new Mezzo.

Chapter Five

Literary Bloomsbury and Fitzrovia

The boundaries of Bloomsbury are rather blurred — from Gower Street to Woburn Place on the east and from Euston Road down to the British Museum on the south is the approximate area, with Russell Square being almost in the centre. The famous Bloomsbury group consisted of writers and poets who lived there; most of them had country retreats as well.

The area called Fitzrovia, which includes Fitzroy Square, runs from Gower Street over to Great Portland Street.

In Fitzroy Square there are two plaques outside the house where George Bernard Shaw and later Virginia Woolf lived; and just around the corner there is another on the town house of Ottoline Morell. It is a peculiarly quaint part of London and it seems that the area was more popular at the beginning of the century. Somerset Maugham's wife Syrie writes about several furniture warehouses in the area, a large one in Fitzroy Square. Today there seems to be no such business or trade in the area, the only shops being on the main thoroughfares, and a few coffee shops and the Samuel French bookshop on Fitzroy Street. Perhaps George Bernard Shaw lived there because of its close proximity to the Reading Room at the British Museum. He was married from this address after Charlotte Payne-Townsend rescued him from ill-health, depression and the terrible mess in his room — books piled up everywhere with the congealed remains of meals on dirty plates; apple cores, dust, papers strewn everywhere and unwashed clothes on the floor. She offered to take care of him if they were together under one roof in the country, so he was concerned enough to tell her she had better go out and obtain a marriage licence as he didn't want her compromised. When the wedding took place, in the pouring rain in Henrietta Street in Covent Garden, the Registrar mistook Shaw for one of the witnesses, he was so poorly dressed, and thought that one of the witnesses, less unkempt, was the groom. Charlotte whisked him away from Fitzroy Square forever.

Another plaque marks the office where T S Eliot worked for a time and it was at the Russell Hotel where many of the Bloomsbury group gathered for their meetings. The Bloomsbury group, once referred to as the Bloomsberries by one of the people on its fringes, Molly MacCarthy, came into being in the first decade of this century, and contained some of the most gifted individuals in modern times. It was a collection of persons who thought of themselves primarily as friends, some related, some married or simply lovers; many of the men were contemporaries at Cambridge. The whole Bloomsbury phenomenon would never have existed without two sisters, Virginia (later Woolf) and Vanessa (later Bell) Stephen, daughters of Sir Leslie Stephen, an eminent Victorian writer who died in 1904.

Vanessa and Virginia, with their brothers Thoby and Adrian, all four in their early twenties, thereupon moved to 46 Gordon Square in Bloomsbury; Thoby had been a close friend and contemporary at Trinity College Cambridge of Clive Bell and Leonard Woolf, later becoming the brother-in-law of both, and also of Lytton Strachey, who once proposed marriage to, and was accepted by, Virginia; the engagement lasted less than twenty-four hours. Clive Bell married Vanessa three years later, in 1907. Leonard Woolf, after a seven year stint in Ceylon as a colonial civil servant, married Virginia in 1912.

Trinity College Cambridge also played a pivotal role in the genesis of the group. Soon after their arrival there, Clive Bell, Leonard Woolf and Lytton Strachey formed a reading club with two other members, A J Robertson and Saxon Sydney-Turner, which they called the Midnight Club simply because they met every Saturday at midnight. It marked however the beginning of the Bloomsbury group although Robertson soon dropped out of both the club and the group. Lytton Strachey also had the distinction of being elected a member of The Apostles, a very exclusive society which in the hundred years of its existence up to that time had had fewer than two hundred and forty members. Other members who became his friends included Maynard Keynes, the economist, Bertrand Russell and G E Moore, both philosophers, E M Forster, the writer, and Desmond MacCarthy, the literary journalist.

Lytton Strachey was the eleventh child of a soldier, Lt-General Sir Richard Strachey who at forty-two married his then nineteen-year old wife, Julia. Duncan Grant, the painter, was his first cousin and also a member of the Bloomsbury group. Lytton was no stranger to eccentricity from his earliest years; one of his father's brothers lived in England by Calcutta time, presumably because he had once been stationed there. Lytton grew up under the care, if you can call it that, of his mother. She seems to have been a domineering and stupid woman who sent him to unsuitable schools where he was a lonely and awkward boy; she tried to send him to Oxford, but fortunately he wasn't accepted, so he went to Cambridge instead.

One should at this point list the members of the Bloomsbury group.

Leonard Woolf wrote: "Bloomsbury did not exist in 1911; it came into existence in the three years 1912 to 1914," and lists those whom he considered to be its members: Vanessa, Virginia and Adrian Stephen (Thoby had died at the age of twenty-six), Desmond and Molly MacCarthy, Maynard Keynes, Clive Bell, E M Forster, Roger Fry, Sydney-Turner, Lytton Strachey, Duncan Grant, Clive Bell and Leonard Woolf, fourteen in all. They were seen as a group of eccentrics, mostly affecting Lytton Strachey's peculiar manner of speaking, wearing unconventional clothes, and tolerating permissive sexual behaviour, including homosexuality, both male and female, and free love both inside and outside marriage. They themselves were proud of two things, their habit of applying reason to every aspect of life, and their creativity. They had little interest in politics as usually conceived; they did not engage in polemics, did not organise or take part in demonstrations, and did not try to proselytise; where they believed that conventional rules of behaviour were unreasonable, they ignored them, but did not flaunt their attitudes. For this reason, they were always well received in the circles into which they had been born. They were not snobs in a narrow social sense, but intolerant of stupidity and lack of intellectual honesty.

Vita Sackville West first met Virginia Woolf at a dinner party given by Clive Bell in London on the 14th December 1922. Soon after, Virginia dined with Vita at her house in Ebury Street, and on 11th January 1923 Vita paid her first visit to Hogarth House, Richmond, where the Woolfs had begun to print short books including T S Eliot's *Wasteland*. Their friendship at first seemed to develop rapidly following her visit to Richmond and Vita wrote to her husband, Harold Nicholson, "I love Mrs Woolf with a sick passion." But it was more inclined to be instant admiration than instant infatuation.

Addresses relating to the Bloomsbury group:

46 Gordon Square. This was the house that the Stephen children(Vanessa, Virginia, Thoby and Adrian) moved into on the death of their father in 1904. Thoby died in 1906.

51 Gordon Square. Home of Lytton Strachey.

29 Fitzroy Square. Virginia and Adrian moved here in 1907 following the marriage of Vanessa to Clive Bell; Clive and Vanessa lived in 46 Gordon Square then. George Bernard Shaw had lived at 29 Fitzroy Square from 1887 to 1898.

33 Fitzroy Square. Roger Fry set up the Omega Workshop here in 1913.

37 Fitzroy Square. Ford Madox Ford gave, from 1865, fortnightly evenings here for eight years to entertain fellow Pre-Raphaelites, political refugees and foreigners. Turgeniev, Liszt, Mark Twain and Cosima Wagner were guests here. Tennyson and Browning also came, and much poetry was recited.

8 Fitzroy Street. This was home to Walter Sickert and before that to Whistler.

38 Brunswick Square. Virginia and Adrian moved here in 1911. Duncan Grant, Maynard Keynes and Leonard Woolf joined them here. Leonard and Virginia married in 1912. The absent-minded Virginia asked a man sitting next to her at dinner whether he was interested in politics; his name was Asquith, and he was Prime Minister at the time.

44 Bedford Square. Lady Ottoline Morrell and her husband Philip Morrell moved here in 1905, a few years after their marriage.

17 Southampton Place. This was the boyhood home of John Cardinal Newman.

37 Mecklenburgh Square. Virginia and Leonard Woolf moved there in 1939, taking with them their Hogarth Press.

52 Tavistock Square. Virginia and Leonard Woolf lived here from 1924 to 1939 and operated the Hogarth Press from here.

CHAPTER SIX

A Visit to Ivor Novello's Flat and a Stroll Down The Strand

Ivor Novello's London Home

Ivor Novello was the first superstar. At twenty-one he was the composer of one of the most popular, and poignant, songs of the First World War — *Keep the Home Fires Burning*. At twenty-six he was a silent movie star. In his thirties he was Britain's biggest male box office draw, and in his thirties he had a string of successful plays in the West End, as both playwright and star.

In his forties he returned to his original love — music — and dominated British musical theatre with a string of smash hits at Drury Lane. He kept this phenomenal workload going through the 1930s and 1940s, and when he died, aged 58, in 1951, he was starring in his musical, *King's Rhapsody*, and had another hit, *Gay's The Word*, which he had written for Cicely Courtneidge, playing in the West End as well.

He seemed to epitomise the glamour, the success, and the sheer enjoyment that theatre — both musical and straight — represented. He had the added advantage that although he was every bit as glamorous as Noel Coward — though less witty — he was, in relation to Coward, relatively unknown to younger generations, so I had the added excitement of feeling that I was discovering an extraordinary secret when I came across his work.

Ivor — as everyone used to call him — devoted his life to the theatre, over and above his love of music, though he combined the two wherever he could. That is why his musicals were such a success; he put all of his remarkable talent, energy and enthusiasm into each production. The title of one of his last songs, a tribute to the Edwardian stars he had watched as a boy, could as easily have applied to him. It was called *Vitality*.

This love of theatre, which I shared, had been expressed in his choice of home. He lived not just in or near theatre-land, but above a theatre (the Strand) in the Aldwych, next door to the Waldorf Hotel, a few yards from the Aldwych Theatre (which hosted the farces written by Ben Travers, a wartime colleague of Ivor's in the Royal Naval Air Service) and opposite the famous Gaiety theatre, which was, sadly, pulled down in the 1950s and turned into offices.

Ivor died nearly fifty years ago, and the world that he represented — the music and the romance of the Edwardian era, the magic of the silent movies, the glamour of the inter-war years with their jazz-age fashion, smart restaurants, beautiful clothes and spectacular musicals, the heroic defiance of German bombs during the War, and his defiant production of lavish all-star shows in the otherwise austere post-war years — seemed to have all disappeared, along with the Gaiety Theatre, the Saville Theatre (where his last show, *Gay's the Word*, had been produced), and the society restaurants like Romano's and the Cafe de Paris.

What was left? A blue plaque, one of the commemorative signs placed on the houses of the famous by English Heritage, has been placed by the door to Ivor's flat. Every time one waits for a red London bus in the Aldwych (usually in the inevitable London rain), the plaque reminds passers-by that Ivor Novello, Actor-Manager and Composer, once lived there.

Ivor had bought the flat in 1913, had died there in March 1951, and it had long since passed out of the hands of his estate. I knew that his loyal friend, Olive Gilbert, for whom he wrote a singing part in all of his musicals, had lived in the flat below him to help keep an eye on him (though he also had servants and his partner, Bobbie Andrews, to do this). But Olive had passed away as well. No doubt that famous home, known to all of theatrical London for forty years as, simply, The Flat, would have been transformed into an office, changed beyond all recognition from those publicity photographs that Ivor had allowed to be taken there.

Purely by chance I discovered that though it was now a suite of offices, it was suitably, the London base of a leading theatrical impresario, Duncan Weldon, whose beautifully produced, star-studded plays at the Theatre Royal, Haymarket, and other such grand venues, would have earned Ivor's approval.

I took my courage in my hands and phoned his office, explaining that I was a theatre historian with a special interest in Ivor Novello, and could I please have a look round what had been his home for so many years? The answer was immediate. Yes!

On the appointed day I rang the bell outside the door to the flat. It was wooden, and old, and would doubtless have been recognised by Ivor. I was lucky — since my visit it has been removed and replaced with a dull, bland, modern piece of glass and chrome.

As the door buzzed open I entered the little hallway and found myself face to face with the famously small and unreliable (though slightly modernised since Ivor's day) lift. As I ascended in this tiny wooden contraption, which on many occasions had threatened to trap numerous celebrities between the floors, I remembered reading Noel Coward's description in his autobiography, *Present Indicative*.

"The Flat" sat, and still sits, on the very top of the Strand Theatre, and, in order to reach it, a perilous ascent was made in this small, self-worked lift. Ivor's guests crushed themselves timorously together in this frightening little box, someone pulled a rope, there was a sharp grinding noise, a scream from some less hardy member of the party, then, swaying and rattling, the box ascended. Upon reaching the top, it would hit the roof with a crash and, more often than not, creak all the way down again. The big room of the flat had a raised dais running across one end. Upon this were sometimes two grand pianos, at other times none; sometimes a gramophone, and nearly always Viola Tree, an actress and close friend. The high spots of the parties were reached in this room. Charades were performed, people did stunts. Olga Lynn sang, and Fay Compton immediately did an imitation of Olga Lynn singing.

When I reached Mr Weldon's offices I was given a free run of the place and, though all signs of the original furnishings had gone, the shape of the rooms, even down to the dais that Coward had referred to, were still there, so the whole place seemed strangely familiar. I would not have asked, but a secretary asked if I would like to go onto the roof. Thus, I even managed to see where Ivor, who loved to sunbathe and, like his friend Noel Coward, had bought a home in Jamaica to avoid the worst of the English winter, had lapped up the sun when in London.

This love of the sun had taken Ivor abroad whenever he had the chance, and his first film, *L'Appel du Sang*, directed by Louis Mercanton, was set in Italy. He had been given the part in 1919, just after the First World War. During the War he had achieved fame and fortune at the age of twenty-one when, in 1914, he wrote *Keep The Home Fires Burning*.

Already a published composer whose work had been performed at the Albert Hall, Ivor decided to write a patriotic song to pre-empt his mother, who had been threatening to compose one herself. Had she been able to write one before her son, the family reputation would never have recovered.

Ivor already had the melody in his head when he invited a young American poetess, called Lena Guilbert Ford, to write the lyrics. It was in the flat above the Aldwych, as Ivor played the tune on the piano, that inspiration struck. It had been a particularly cold day, and as Ivor and Lena sat together, the maid came in and laid some fresh logs in the fireplace.

"That's it!" he cried, "Keep the Home Fires Burning!" He

32

immediately wrote down the words of the chorus, and Lena wrote the verses. Sadly, she was not able to benefit from their joint effort as she and her baby were killed during a Zeppelin raid on London.

Ivor tried for an air career, but after two plane crashes his commanding officer decided that he was causing more damage than the Luftwaffe, so he was seconded to a desk job in Whitehall. This was highly convenient for him, not only because he was a short walk from his flat in the Aldwych, but because he was within walking distance of the West End, where his songs were appearing in a number of revues and musical shows.

It was, therefore, as a composer that he was famous in 1919, when Louis Mercanton approached a casting agency, looking for a handsome, dark-haired young man to play the role of a hot blooded Latin lover in his new film. It did not take Mercanton long to spot the soon-to-be-famous Novello profile. "That's the man!" he exclaimed, and, when told that the boy was a composer, not an actor, he refused to be put off.

Ivor's background and professional live was in music, but the theatre was the great love of his life, and he jumped at the chance to be an actor. True, his performances were on the silver screen rather than the stage, but silent movies required highly theatrical acting (and make-up), so this was an excellent introduction to an acting career; besides which, how many young men, without any drama school training are offered the lead role in a glamorous French movie as a first job?

Ivor's later career as actor/manager/composer, with a string of hit musicals to his name, saw him cast as either an Englishman (albeit in lavish foreign surroundings) a Viennese composer or a Ruritanian King. Attempts to play Italians were abandoned after his disastrous appearance in Noel Coward's 1927 play, *Sirocco*.

Not one of Coward's best plays, it had taken a great deal to persuade Novello (who knew his limitations) to accept the part of a sultry young Italian. The first-night audience took an immediate dislike to Coward's play in general, and hissing noises were made from the gallery, along with increasingly loud and frequent ad-libs to the text. When Ivor's character sulkily claimed that he was about to go to his mother, a ribald response from the gods suggested what he might like to do when he got there!

The play was to go into West End history as a synonym for disaster. Noel Coward's mother, whose deafness had been the prime cause for her son's adoption of his famously clipped tones, turned to her son and asked nervously: "Is it a failure, dear?". Coward by name, courageous by nature, he was determined to face out the audience's dislike of the performance.

To be fair, not everybody was against it, and the physical blows that were swapped between his supporters and his detractors enlivened the proceedings in the stalls.

All this culminated in the curtain call, when Ivor and his leading lady, Frances Doble, led the cast in bows that met with a storm of abuse from the enraged patrons in the gallery. The stage manager, almost as deaf as Mrs Coward, took the catcalls and boos for signs of enthusiasm and kept ringing the curtain up for yet another bow. It was the custom, in those days, for the author not only to take a first-night curtain call, but to make a speech of thanks, to cast and audience, from the stage. Before he could say anything, France Doble, by now in a state of hysterics, stepped forward to give her curtain speech, too shocked to say anything other than the speech that she had prepared earlier in anticipation of the usual Noel Coward first-night success.

"Ladies and gentlemen," she stuttered, to renewed tirades of abuse, "This is the happiest night of my life..." The play soon closed, and Ivor and Noel's friendship survived the most traumatic theatrical failure of either man's career.

Coward followed Kipling's famous exhortation in *If,* by treating disaster and triumph in the same way — he got on a ship and sailed away. Whether it was to celebrate a success or flee from a failure, to recuperate from illness, to overcome one of the nervous breakdowns that afflicted him as a young man, or simply to recharge his batteries, Coward loved to get in a ship and steam off into the sunset.

Ivor joined him in buying a house in Jamaica, which in the 1940s was a fashionable place to go for the sunshine — Lord Beaverbrook, the newspaper magnate, was a neighbour and friend on the island. Ivor sailed a lot less than Noel, though he had enjoyed his fair share of transatlantic trips in the days when it was the only practical way to travel to and from New York.

On one occasion he had been due to sail home from the States, only to find that the stray dog that he had adopted was missing. Refusing his friends' request to leave the wretched dog to its own devices, he postponed sailing until, after a day or two's delay, the dog turned up. Ivor's famous generosity and kindness worked in his favour on this occasion, for the ship that he had been due to sail on was involved in an accident that led to its sinking a little way out of New York, with the loss of hundreds of lives.

He did not let this incident put him off cruising, however, and ocean liners were to be a feature of several of his spectacular 1930s musicals. In a radio interview in later life, he described how his parents' home in Cardiff had been the centre of musical and theatrical life in the city, that he had grown up surrounded by beautifully dressed stars, and that this had given him a taste for glamour that had stayed with him all his life. Ocean liners were then (and still are, despite the social changes of the intervening sixty years) seen as the epitome of glamour, so it is appropriate than one featured strongly in the first of his Drury Lane shows, the aptly named *Glamorous Night*, in 1935.

This has as its hero a young English television inventor, who travels to a remote country named Krasnia in search of fame and fortune. Ivor's musicals were heavily influenced by those of Lehar and other Edwardian composers whose work Ivor had seen as a young man, and despite the inclusion of some very topical themes — after all, television was in its infancy in 1935 — his musicals are very much in the Viennese operetta tradition.

Having arrived in Krasnia, Ivor saves a famous opera singer played by the American star, Mary Ellis, (whose own career began in the New York Met during the First World War) from assassination. The reason for the assassination attempt is that Mary is not just an opera star, she is the King of Krasnia's mistress!

One of the themes of Ivor's shows was the importance of duty and doing the right social and moral thing, so in order to save her royal lover from further embarrassment, Mary goes on a cruise — as does Ivor, who has fallen for her charms. As you would expect, both of a cruise ship, and of a Novello musical, the liner is the last word in luxury and romance, even running to a stunningly beautiful stowaway in the shape of the black American cabaret star, Elizabeth Welch. Miss Welch sings a shanty but is otherwise unengaged, as the ship swiftly proceeds to sink, providing an astonished first-night audience with a spectacular special effect, using all the technical resources of the vast Drury Lane stage.

Once shipwrecked, Ivor and Mary land safely ashore and discover a gypsy encampment, where they are made welcome. Gypsies are something of a running theme through Novello's career. In one of his early silent movie successes, *The Bohemian Girl*, in which he starred opposite the young Gladys Cooper, he plays a Polish nobleman who is similarly sheltered, in his hour of need, by a troop of gypsies, improbably led by that epitome of upper-class elderly English gents, C Aubrey Smith!

This being a Novello production, the gypsies in *Glamorous Night* are a highly romantic group, and when Ivor and Mary decide to have a gypsy wedding, their new-found friends find them stunningly beautiful wedding clothes, and themselves appear at the ceremony in gorgeous national costume covered in brocade and dripping with semi-precious stones!

Glamorous Night received the rare accolade of a visit by King George V and Queen Mary. The King was not keen on music, an area in which his tastes were philistine, to say the least. When asked for the name of his favourite opera, he replied that it was *La Bohème* — "Because it's the shortest"— and, when asked the name of his favourite tune, he said, without a second's delay, *"God Save the King"*. Despite the show's royal stamp of approval, the owners of Drury Lane had hedged their bets by booking in a pantomime for the winter, so *Glamorous Nights* had a surprisingly short run. The following year Ivor pulled off another success, with *Careless Rapture*, a wide-ranging show that involved Chinese brigands, oriental temples and a full-scale earthquake on-stage. In 1937, he had been asked to insert another scene at sea, and he duly obliged. Having portrayed, and then sunk an ocean liner in *Glamorous Nights* he felt he had to do something a little different this time round, so he put in a transformation scene in which the liner was transformed into a battleship!

At the end of each night's performance at the Theatre Royal, he would be mobbed by legions of fans, mostly female, outside the stage door. These days many stars are not prepared to meet their public, or to do more than a bare minimum of autograph signing before being whisked away by bodyguards and limousines.

In the 1930s there was still a tradition that stars owed a duty to their public, and Novello was famous throughout theatre land not just for his good nature and ready, matinee-idol smile, but for his attention to his fans. Every night, once he had greeted the celebrities, (those British like Noel Coward and Gladys Cooper, or visiting Americans like Joan Crawford and Douglas Fairbanks Jnr) who crowded into his dressing room, he would appear at the stage door and sign as many autographs as necessary, his profile lit to full advantage by the stage door light, before being driven the few hundred yards home to the Aldwych in his Rolls Royce with the monogrammed doors.

The last of his shows to be presented at Drury Lane was *The Dancing Years*, which opened in 1939. The Lane was taken over, for the duration of the war, by the armed forces' entertainment agency, ENSA— affectionately known to the troops as "Every Night Something Awful". *The Dancing Years* spent the war years on tour and at the Adelphi Theatre in The Strand. It was while he was starring in *The Dancing Years* at the Adelphi that Ivor served a month's prison sentence in Wormwood Scrubs, a notorious north London jail.

The cause of this extraordinary sentence was his beloved Rolls Royce, which transported him back to the Flat during the week, and down to the country house, Redroofs, at the weekend. Strict petrol rationing made this impossible, but a woman fan, who claimed to work in a senior capacity at a firm based in Maidenhead, near Redroofs, appeared to have found a legal way round this problem.

Unfortunately, it turned out that her obsession with Ivor had got the better of her, for she was employed as a clerk, with no authority to arrange deals between her firm and Ivor. When this came to light Ivor was charged with conspiring to break the law. The government wanted a rich and famous scapegoat to make an example of, and although the normal punishment would have been a fine (as Noel Coward found when he broke the currency laws) Ivor was sentenced to jail.

This mean-spirited and spiteful gesture backfired terribly, for the sentence was so clearly unjust that the public reaction was very much in Novello's favour, and when he returned to the stage of the Adelphi after his month's absence, there was a storm of applause, and cheering from the audience, who confirmed his place as the King of the West End musical.

Although his reputation survived, his health was broken by the experience and so, according to many friends, was his spirit. Having spent his life in music and the theatre, a beautiful and talented man surrounded by the most attractive and gifted people in London, creating superb plays, films and musicals for several decades, the shock of being thrown into prison was appalling. He survived, and wrote two more spectacular musicals, *Perchance to Dream* (1945) and *King's Rhapsody* (1949), but his health, which had never been very strong and had not been helped by his habit of chain-smoking cigarettes throughout his adult life, was permanently weakened, and he died while still in his professional prime.

His very last show was *Gay's The Word*, written for his old friend, Cicely Courtneidge. She had been a musical star and comedienne since the First World War, thanks partly to the fact that her father, Robert Courtneidge was a leading impresario of the late Victorian and Edwardian eras, and thanks partly to her stage partnership with her husband, Jack Hulbert.

Cicely's career had been in decline, and Ivor, whose generosity had already been referred to, promised to write the music for a show with which to revive her fortunes. His usual lyricist was the immensely talented Christopher Hassall, but for this show he teamed up with Alan Melville, whose witty lyrics were perfectly suited to this light hearted piece.

The show's main character is a retired star of the Gaiety theatre, the bastion of Edwardian musicals that stood exactly opposite Ivor's flat, on the other side of the Aldwych. Sadly the theatre has since been pulled down for office development. All that is left of this glorious building, outside whose stage door top-hatted Edwardian men-about-town used to wait for the Gaiety girls, before escorting them into their carriages and off to supper at one of the innumerable society restaurants, is a simple plaque whose presence reminds us of another London theatre that has been lost forever.

Gay's the Word's central character is called Gay Daventry (hence the title) and she sings a song about herself, called *Gaiety Glad*. Cicely Courtneidge's best-known song from this show, however, was a number called *Vitality*, which she adopted as her theme song for the rest of her career. In *Vitality*, she recalls the great names of the Edwardian stage many of whose careers, like those of Phyllis and Zena Dare, had been given a second lease of life through Ivor's shows. The song is a celebration of British musical talent that is both affectionately nostalgic and defiantly defensive, as in the line: "Give me Gracie Fields instead of any crooner". The fact that it was Ivor's last show makes it all the more poignant, and many people can still remember the first night, when a clearly ill but still sun-tanned and elegant Ivor appeared in a box at the Saville theatre to watch Cicely Courtneidge's triumph. At the curtain call the audience spontaneously turned to him and applauded, but in a characteristic gesture he waved his arm at the stage and told them their cheers should be for the star, not the composer.

In one of the countless press interviews that he gave in the course of his nearly forty years at the top, Ivor was asked how he wanted to die. His reply was very specific — that it should be on stage, at the end of a curtain call speech after a tremendous success starring in one of his own musicals, with the applause still ringing in his ears. Apart from the ghastly injustice and humiliation of a month in prison, his life was one glittering success after another, and he was granted a death that only missed this ideal scenario by a few hours.

On March 5th, 1951, he had appeared as usual, in *King's Rhapsody*, one of his best musicals, in which he played the Crown Prince, and subsequently King, of a Ruritanian country. He had been determined to fight back against the post-war fashion for American blockbusters by writing a defiantly old-fashioned English musical, with kings and queens, twenty-one gun salutes, ballrooms and jewels, and the trademark, lush Novello music, full of show-stopping songs and memorable melodies.

His leading lady was an unknown that he had discovered, employed, and promoted — Vanessa Lee. He had even changed her name, from her real one, Ruby Moule, to Vanessa Lee. He had thought the name Vanessa suited her character, and having worked in the West End with the young Vivien Leigh (née Hartley), he decided that the surname — spelt differently, of course — would bring her luck. Among the other women in the show were several of his old favourites, the Dare sisters (Zena playing his mother, Phyllis playing his mistress!) and Olive Gilbert, who, with Muriel Barron, had been the first to sing Ivor's most popular tune, *We'll Gather Lilacs*, in *Perchance to Dream*. Olive, a stout lady with a superb contralto voice, was one of Ivor's closest friends, and supervised the staff at his Aldwych flat, as well as generally ensuring that everything in his off-stage life was comfortable and properly arranged. She had the little flat beneath his, and was summoned upstairs in the early hours of the morning on 6th March.

Ivor had returned home after the show, in the company of his producer Tom Arnold, a highly talented man who produced a whole range of entertainments, from Ivor's musicals to ice shows and pantomimes. After the inevitable bottle of champagne, he had left, though he was concerned at the twinges of pain that Ivor felt in his chest.

After midnight the pains returned, and Ivor's friend, Bobbie Andrews, who lived with him, called Olive upstairs, A doctor was called for, but he could do nothing, and as he, Olive and Bobbie stood, helpless, Ivor passed gently away from a heart attack. True, he had not died exactly as he would have wished, but he had had another hugely successful evening in the lead of his own show, had celebrated with his old friend and business partner, and died in his beloved Aldwych flat with two of the people he was closest to at his side.

Just as the Gaiety theatre and the way of life that it represented has been reduced to a small plaque on a dreary modern wall, so the life of one of the most extraordinarily talented men of the London stage and the British cinema, who kept the British musical theatre alive over twenty years, has been reduced to a neat little plaque over an anonymous looking doorway behind an Aldwych bus stop. But though it may mean little to tourists waiting for transport to St Paul's Cathedral or office workers going home after a long day's work, to anyone with any knowledge of or interest in theatre and music, that plaque, and the flat that it refers to, is shorthand for the glamour, spectacle and style of Ivor Novello.

The Savoy

This theatre was conceived by and built for Richard D'Oyly Carte with the express purpose of staging the Gilbert and Sullivan operettas which he had produced with such success for many years. It opened in 1881 and was the first theatre in London to be lit by electricity. It was built on the Embankment in the grounds of the former Savoy Palace Hotel, the predecessor of the present Savoy Hotel, and the entrance was originally on the Embankment. For the first fifteen years almost nothing other than the Gilbert and Sullivan operas were played there, subsequently there were a few seasons of revivals. With the exception of a few other musicals, notably Noel Coward's *Sail Away* and a musical version of his *Blithe Spirit*, it has been, with the exception of its early days, the home of legitimate theatre

Its best-known patron was probably Winston Churchill who usually occupied the Royal Box. Many other famous names are associated with the theatre; Harley Granville-Barker, better known now as a playwright, produced in the years before the first World War two seasons of Shakespeare's plays which were extremely well received. Noel Coward had several of his plays done there, including *The Young Idea* in which he also played. Laurence Olivier starred in *Journey's End* in 1929. Robert Morley, starring in *The Man Who Came to Dinner* brought the play the fame that it so richly deserved. Margaret Lockwood had a two year run in the 1950s in *The Spider's Web*. One could go on and on; the Savoy remains one of the favourite theatres for Londoners.

The Strand

Almost too extravagant in both its architecture and its interior decoration, the Strand Theatre was built in 1905, and has been operating non-stop since then in spite of being bombed in both world wars; on neither occasion were the performances more than briefly interrupted. Celebrated plays produced there for the first time include *A Funny Thing Happened on the Way to the Forum* which ran for two years, and *No Sex Please We're British* which ran for eleven. *Cabaret* ran for a year, and Tom Stoppard's *The Real Thing* also had its first production there. *Arsenic and Old Lace* ran for a couple of years during the Second World War. Charles Laughton played in *Bachelor Father* in 1927, before he started his film career.

The Vaudeville

This is the West End theatre par excellence, producing mostly light entertainment since its opening in 1870; however at its inception, Henry Irving, then relatively obscure at the age of thirty-two, was employed to play in a light comedy *Two Roses*. Julian Slade's *Salad Days* was first played here and ran for six years. William Douglas Home wrote *The Chiltern Hundreds* which was produced here in 1947 and ran for two years. While some serious plays have been seen here, general speaking, revues and comedies have been its mainstays.

Chapter Seven

Following in Noel Coward's Footsteps

Among the hundreds of celebrities that the last hundred years has produced, only two are so well known that their very name sums up an era. They are Oscar Wilde and Noel Coward. The very term "an Oscar Wilde type" or "very Noel Coward" when used of an individual, immediately sums up a mental image of how that person looks, acts and, above all, talks.

Both men share a reputation for wit, Wilde's of an occasionally florid and arch variety, Coward's as clipped as his famous delivery. If Wilde's name conjures up images of the Cafe Royal, hansom cabs, the St James' theatre and the London of Dorian Gray, then Coward's provides us with silk dressing gowns, cigarette holders and Riviera balconies. His personification of the inter-war years is best expressed in his marvellous tunes. As he himself wrote, cheap music can be very potent, and his popular tunes, whether the jazz age classics like *Dance Little Lady* and *Room with A View*, or *London Pride*, that hymn to the defiant spirit that saw his home town through the Blitz, can still sum up in a couple of chords far more than pages and pages of history textbooks.

Despite his remarkable work on behalf of the war effort from 1939 to 1945, that saw him tour the Empire giving innumerable concerts to battle-weary troops; and, above all, despite his superb film, *In Which We Serve*, which immortalised the exploits of his friend, Lord Louis Mountbatten, and his ship (*The Kelly*) and crew, despite all this and the immediate post-war success of *Brief Encounter*, one of the most powerfully romantic movies ever made, Coward fell out of critical favour. This, combines with the exigencies of the Labour government's taxation policies, led him to seek work — and a home — overseas.

Yet before this drastic wrench from a nation which he seemed to symbolise to the outside world, and whose stiff upper lip he had affectionately satirised in *Mad Dogs and Englishmen*, Coward had lived, worked and, above all, partied, in a Belgravia studio apartment, number 17 Gerald Road. The flat was located in one of the smartest residential areas of the capital, among the vast estates of the Duke of Westminster, the richest landowner in Britain, and the wealthiest individual after the King. It was typical of Noel's sense of humour, and ability to poke fun at the aristocratic world that he so much enjoyed being a part of, that he should write the tongue-in-cheek song, *The Stately Homes of England*, and, more particularly, that he should include his landlord in one of the best known lines of one of his best known plays — *Private Lives*: "Whose yacht is that in the harbour? The Duke of Westminster's. It usually is."

Despite his glamorous image, Noel had been born to lower middle class parents in the pleasant but distinctly unfashionable suburb of Teddington. In 1918, the last year of the First World War, and the year which saw Noel's brief and inglorious service in the armed forces (he was invalided out, suffering from nervous strain) his parents moved to 111 Ebury Road.

This house, tall and substantial, was in fact a lodging house, and they were forced to take in paying guests in order to make ends meet. Around the corner from Victoria Station, Ebury Road was technically in Pimlico. Noel's future home, in Gerald Road, was not far away in geographical terms, but was a lifetime away in terms of cost and social standing.

111 Ebury Street still stands today and, appropriately enough, is now a hotel, run by two men, whose framed advertisement outside the hotel proudly announces that this was once the home of Noel Coward. While he lived there, Noel had the attic room, so that the better ones could be let, profitably, to genteel strangers. As he became established as a playwright and composer, he was increasingly able to afford to relieve his mother of the necessity to let so many rooms, so, as he once quipped to a friend, he must have been the only person in the world who moved downwards as his career moved upwards.

The fact that his father (who had been a piano salesman in happier times) was ineffective as a wage earner by the time the family moved to Ebury Street, was not entirely unwelcome to Noel. Like any young man would have been, he was proud of his ability to provide for himself at an early age and, as the '20s progressed and his career moved with them, he became the breadwinner of the family. A source of pride to any dutiful son, this fact gave extra pleasure to him, due to the intense and mutual devotion between determined, proud mother and talented, affectionate son.

Noel's mother, Violet, had been the traditional stage mother, determined that her son should succeed as a child actor and singer. However much hope she may have had, she cannot, of course, have known until later that her faith in her son as a prodigy of the stage would be justified. Nevertheless, her hopes were to be wildly exceeded as the not particularly attractive but distinctly self-confident boy was to prove himself one of the giants of British theatre, and of popular music and cinema, too.

Given the close parallels between their careers, quite apart from their friendship and their shared homosexuality, it is fascinating to note that both Noel Coward and Ivor Novello — who, in their different ways, dominated the British stage for several decades — had extraordinary and determined mothers who to a large degree made their respective careers possible.

Noel's mother was a determined woman without any particular theatrical connections. Ivor's was a world famous singing teacher and choir mistress who had been granted a royal title for her choir by Queen Victoria herself. Mrs Novello Davies, known to Ivor and his friends as "Mam", had also carved out a career as a teacher on both sides of the Atlantic, and had won prizes and competitions in North America as well as in her native Wales.

Like Mrs Coward, she had lost her first child (though hers had been a girl while Noel's elder sibling had been a boy) and seemed all the more determined for her next one not only to survive, but to succeed, to compensate for the pain of the lost life that had gone before. Mam had been determined that her son would be a musician, and she fiercely resisted Ivor's attempts to go on stage. Violet Coward had no such qualms, and positively encouraged Noel in that direction. Although, like Mam, Violet had a docile and uncomplaining husband, she had no career (other than the drudgery of running Ebury Street) of her own, so she had to live her life almost entirely through Noel.

Despite this, and the correspondingly strong bond between them (strengthened by the fact that there was never going to be a woman in Noel's personal life to come between them), Noel wanted to have his own space. Thus, as soon as he felt he could afford it, following successes on both sides of the Atlantic, he moved a few streets away — but across a social chasm — to number 17, Gerald Road, in 1930. He was celebrating a new decade, for both the century and himself, by becoming his own master.

Today there is a large blue plaque on the gatepost outside the house, announcing that it was Noel's home for over twenty years. His home was a converted coach house that was reached through an arch formed by the neighbouring property. This meant that it had that vital qualification for any hard-pressed celebrity — privacy from the prying eyes of the public.

Prying ears were another matter, however, for despite being set away from the road, the noise generated by Noel's pre-war parties frequently disturbed his neighbours, one of whom was the local police station! Noel was always good at charming the constabulary, whether in London or

New York, and he never wrote a song that poked fun of them, but this was one issue on which he had more than his fair share of brushes with the law.

When he was not making whoopee with friends, the house had the advantage of peace and quiet as well as privacy, and this was a further point in its favour, as he used to enjoy an afternoon siesta between lunch at the Ivy or some similarly fashionable establishment, and an evening of cocktails and laughter, trips to the theatre and cinema, gossip with friends and yet another visit to a well-known restaurant.

The only choice for interior decorator was Somerset Maugham's wife, Syrie, who had become famous as an interior decorator for her love of black and white — very pre-war. Coward's own taste in interior furnishings was notoriously suburban, and visitors to Firefly in Jamaica and Les Avants in Switzerland were often surprised at the unpretentious homeliness of the decor. Homeliness was not, however, a charge that could be levelled at Gerald Road. It was smart, chic, and theatrical in effect, without losing the feel of being a home where one could be comfortable, as well as being a suitably fashionable setting for the beautiful people of the 1930s to meet and enjoy themselves in.

On any given occasion one might expect to find home-grown celebrities like Lilian Braithwaite and her daughter, Joyce Carey, Larry Olivier and Vivien Leigh (not yet married but obviously in love), Ivor Novello, of course, and other leading lights of the theatre aristocracy like John Gielgud, members of the real aristocracy such as Lord Amherst, and royals like the Duke of Kent, with whom Noel once had an affair. From abroad came the likes of Joan Crawford and her husband, Douglas Fairbanks Jnr.

As Noel's theatrical success continued during the decade, so did the profusion of parties. A year after moving into Gerald Road he had one of his greatest hits with *Cavalcade* at the Theatre Royal, Drury Lane. So pleased was he with the public's reaction to this saga of family life that spanned the years from the Boer War to the First World War, that he changed his telegraphic address from Playbrit to Cavalcade, as if to crown himself with his most spectacular and patriotic, achievement.

This core of patriotism, and identification with, and celebration of the normal people of the country — despite his own image of wealth and social contacts at the very highest level — is a fundamental aspect of Noel Coward's personality, and accounts for much of his contemporary success and posthumous affection.

Although he longed to escape from Ebury Street to Gerald Road, he could never forget (nor, to do him credit, did he want to) that he came from Pimlico, not Belgravia. This identification with the man in the street gave him an enormous strength and versatility as a writer, meaning that although he could produce the brittle social comedy of adultery and epigrams that suited Gerald Road and its neighbours, he was also able to write for the Ebury Street lodgers and their families, celebrating old-fashioned values of patriotism and courage (*In Which We Serve*), and the values of old-fashioned morality despite life's more romantic temptations (*Brief Encounter*).

Noel once contemptuously recorded of Ivor's last show, *Gay's The Word* (1951) that it "stank of bad taste…it was rapturously received by a full house." It could never be said that *Cavalcade* was in bad taste. Even at the time, it was seen by some as old-fashioned, an appeal to values that were already dated. After the war, this feeling that Noel was out of touch intensified, which was all the more of a blow to him given the effort he had spent on keeping up morale during the war, and the pride with which his songs had celebrated the joint enterprise against a common enemy — an enemy whom he mercilessly attacked, using his customary wit, in *Don't Let's Be Beastly To The Germans*.

The class warfare that replaced the struggle for survival appalled Coward, though not as much as the taxes that the Labour government levied in order to create the Welfare State. Gerald Road seemed not only a symbol of an England that was passing before his eyes, it was also a financial liability. In order to avoid British income tax he had to move abroad, a move he was able to make thanks to a new career as a cabaret star in America, both in the relatively new medium of television, and on cabaret stages.

This cabaret work had come about partly as a result of his introducing Marlene Dietrich to post-war cabaret audiences. If she could still exert the old-time magic in front of a live audience (despite having no singing voice to speak of), then he was determined that he would demonstrate that he could too. The deciding factor, however, was not so much professional pride but more the financial attractions. Las Vegas, which loved his over-the-top Englishness and thrilled to his racy rendition of Cole Porter's *Let's Do It, Let's Fall In Love*, paid him a small fortune each week for the privilege of hearing *Mad Dogs and Englishmen*. It was with genuine feeling, rather than cynical intent, that Noel wrote and sang *I Like America*.

Although he was to return to England to work, he was, from the early 1950s, an exile. True, he had the rare privilege of enjoying a critical re-evaluation within his own lifetime, largely thanks to his old protégé, Laurence Olivier, asking The Master to direct *Hay Fever* at the National Theatre in 1964, but, although — like the Queen Mother, with whom he enjoyed lunching — he was accorded the honorary status of a National Institution, Gerald Road was his last real English home.

He is buried where he died, in his holiday home in Jamaica. This was partly a romantic gesture — like Robin Hood, he had asked to be buried wherever he died — and partly a symbol of the peace that he had found in that beautiful, lush, Caribbean countryside with its view of one of the great loves of his life, the open sea. And yet one cannot help but feel that this choice was also a silent and everlasting reproach to his homeland for waiting until he was seventy before giving him the knighthood that he had so clearly earned a quarter of a century before. Perhaps if the country that he had loved so much had been a little kinder, if the persecution and shame that he had always feared, as a homosexual, had not been so viciously visited on friends and acquaintances who shared his sexuality, if his success had not been envied and his popularity so easily dismissed by "highbrow" critics, then he might well have been laid to rest among his own people, and in the city he loved so much. He would have been pleased to know that a plaque to his memory was laid in the splendid surroundings of Westminster Abbey, but I am sure he would have preferred, above all else, to have been able to continue to share his hospitality and his home in Gerald Road, where "what has been is past forgetting".

Most of his plays were presented at the Phoenix Theatre in Charing Cross Road and this was where his seventieth birthday celebration was held, attended by well-known theatre personalities as well as by Princess Margaret and Lord Snowdon.

The bar in the Phoenix Theatre is dedicated to his memory, and contains many photographs of him.

To follow actually in his footsteps, you would have only to go from the Phoenix Theatre down to the Ivy Restaurant, his favourite spot for lunch, or carry on down to the Savoy Grill at the Savoy Hotel. In his poem, *The Boy Actors*, he wrote a line about walking down The Strand holding his mother's hand after attending an audition as a very young man.

He also frequented Rules in Maiden Lane and Simpsons in the Strand.

Chapter Eight

Famous Theatrical Restaurants in London

A Theatrical Feast

Prologue to George Farquhar's *The Inconstant, or The Way to Win Him*, at Drury Lane

Like hungry guests a sitting audience looks,
Plays are like suppers: poets are the cooks.
The founders you; the table is this place.
The carvers we, the prologue is the grace.
Each act, a course; each scene, a different dish.
Though we're in Lent, I doubt you're still for flesh—
Satire's the sauce, high-seasoned, sharp, and rough:
Kind masques and beaux, I hope you're pepper-proof.
Wit is the wine; but 'tis so scarce the true,
Poets, like vintners, balderdash and brew.

Your surly scenes, where rant and bloodshed join,
Are butcher's meat, a battle's a sirloin.
Your scenes of love, so flowing, soft, and chaste,
Are water-gruel, without salt or taste.
Bawdy's fat venison, which, too stale, can please;
Your rakes love hogoes like your damned French cheese.
Your rarity for the fair guests to gape on
Is your nice squeaker, or Italian capon;
Or your French virgin-pullet, garnished round
And dressed with sauce of some — four hundred pound.

An opera, like an olio, nicks the age;
Farce is the hasty-pudding of the stage.
For when you're treated with indifferent cheer,
Ye can dispense with slender stage-coach fare.
A pastoral's whipped cream; stage-whims, mere trash;
And tragi-comedy, half fish, half flesh.
But comedy, that, that's the darling cheer.
This night we hope you'll an Inconstant bear;
Wild fowl is liked in playhouse all the year.

Yet since each mind betrays a different taste,
And every dish scarce pleases every guest,
If ought you relish, do not damn the rest.
This favour craved, up let the music strike:
You're welcome all — now fall to where you like!

Peter Motteux (1702)

Rules, 35 Maiden Lane — off Southampton Street, Covent Garden

Throughout its long history the tables of Rules have been crowded with writers, artists, lawyers, journalists and actors. As well as being frequented by great literary talents — including Charles Dickens, William Makepeace Thackeray, John Galsworthy and H G Wells — Rules has also appeared in novels by Rosamond Lehmann, Evelyn Waugh, Graham Greene, John Le Carré, Dick Francis, Penelope Lively and Claire Rayner.

The actors and actresses who have passed through Rules are legion. Down the decades Rules has been an unofficial "Green Room" for the world of entertainment from Henry Irving to Laurence Olivier, and the history of the English stage adorns the walls. The sibling art of the cinema has contributed its own distinguished list of names including those of Buster Keaton, Charles Laughton, Clark Gable, Charlie Chaplin and John Barrymore.

The past lives on at Rules and can be seen on the walls all around you — captured in literally hundreds of drawings, paintings and cartoons. The late John Betjeman, then Poet Laureate, described the ground floor interior as "unique and irreplaceable, and part of literary and theatrical London".

The King Edward Room, an intimate, velvet-swagged room on the first floor, by the lattice window, was once the most celebrated "Table for Two" in London. This was the Prince of Wales' favourite spot for wining and dining the beautiful actress Lily Langtry. So frequent were his visits that Rules put in a special door to enable the Prince to enter and leave without having to walk through the restaurant. Their signed portraits still hang on the walls.

The Charles Dickens Room, a private dining room, is named after the writer who has pride of place in the restaurant's private pantheon because his association with Rules was so poignant. As a young boy he often wandered hungry through the streets and alleys of Covent Garden, his wage from the blacking factory allowing him only a sniff of the mouthwatering aromas that rose from the kitchens. He never forgot those hard times, even when he could afford to enjoy the restaurant later in his life. Rules' memorabilia include playbills for performances of *"Not So Bad As We Seem* and *Mr Nightingale's Diary*, which Dickens produced and performed in, and which he brought to the restaurant himself.

The Greene Room is of course named after Graham Greene, a voluntary exile from Britain who spent much of his life in the South of France, but who still chose to spend all his birthdays in the quintessentially British surroundings of Rules. He was certain to visit the restaurant whenever he returned to London, and it features in several of his books including *The End of the Affair*. Letters from Greene and his sister Elizabeth are displayed on the walls of the Greene Room, bearing witness to Rules' long and happy association with the man widely considered to be Britain's greatest twentieth century writer.

Rules serves the traditional food of this country at its best. It specialises in classic game cookery, oysters, pies and puddings. Rules is fortunate in owning an estate in the High Pennines, "England's last wilderness", which supplies game for the restaurant. Reservations are essential; phone 0171-836-5314.

The Ivy — West Street, off Cambridge Circus

A well-known eating place for theatre/media/publishing people. It has a long history of association with famous stars of the '20s and '30s. Mario Gallati, the head waiter, was a friend of Noel Coward and Ivor Novello. Throughout the twenties he became friends with Gertie Lawrence, Bea Lillie, Winston Churchill, Pavlova, and Dame Marie Tempest. He then started his own restaurant, Le Caprice in Arlington Street, just down from the Ritz in 1947. His book *Gallati at the Caprice* is full of anecdotes about famous people and what they ate, life at the Ivy, followed by life at Le Caprice.

When Noel Coward was first trying to interest producers in his work, he began lunching regularly at the Ivy. He could ill afford it and the owner was kind enough to allow him credit. They became great friends. He describes a particular occasion, not apparently untypical, in 1927, when he had two flops in the same year. The first was *Home Chat* followed almost immediately by *Sirocco* which was an absolute disaster. He was sitting in the stalls with his mother on the first night of *Sirocco* and was painfully aware of the reaction of the audience, which was unsympathetic, to say the least. The audience laughed and booed throughout the play and afterwards, at the stage door, the crowd insulted him and some even spat at him to such an extent that he wrote that he had to send out his jacket to be cleaned the next day. Even his mother, who was usually unaware of any difficulties, sensed that the play was not being well received. They had taken dinner at the Ivy before the performance without any intimation of what was going to happen.

The next day the reviews were so bad that Coward contemplated leaving the city or even the country until the storm blew over; however he decided to brazen it out and went, as usual, to the Ivy for lunch the next day.

He sat at his usual table, not sure of what to expect. However the atmosphere was friendly and quietly sympathetic; he commented that no actors or actresses came over to revile him and the maitre d' in a rare gesture gave him two drinks on the house.

When you go to the Ivy, they will point out his table inside the door.

Le Caprice in Arlington Street

Le Caprice in Arlington Street was opened by Mario Gallati in 1947 when he had retired from the Ivy. Many of his friends, including Ivor Novello, helped him financially so that he could open his own restaurant. It is still the fashionable place to be seen. In his book Mario recounts many stories and anecdotes. One lunch-time, sitting along the wall at different tables were Orson Welles, Robert Morley, Wolf Mankowitz, the late Oliver Hardy of Laurel and Hardy fame, and portly Henry Sherek — quite an impressive sight. Orson Welles is reputed to have called over to Mario and said, "Mario, whatever else you may say, THIS side of the restaurant is a fine advertisement for Caprice food." Whenever Charlie Chaplin came to London Mario knew he would dine at Le Caprice as he had known Mario ever since he had started out as a waiter at Romano's. Coward liked to order aioli (mayonnaise with juice of garlic). He would please Coward enormously with a bowl of bouillabaisse with aioli served in the middle of it.

Mario's book is full of famous names from Pablo Picasso to Maria Callas who dined at Le Caprice. His chapter on what they all ate is interesting, and includes all their favourite dishes and requests. Maria Callas always started with caviar followed by a small steak with lots of green salad and green vegetables.

Vivien Leigh liked French vegetables, especially fennel; baby lamb was also a favourite, and it was Lord Olivier's too.

Terence Rattigan liked steak and kidney pudding for lunch and was also very keen on plovers' eggs.

Clients may be surprised to know that the kitchens of Le Caprice are larger than the restaurant itself. This, of course, is at it should be, for the kitchens of a first-class restaurant are a real world below stairs.

The Grill Room at the Cafe Royal in Regent Street

This is just north of Piccadilly Circus and is, according to the late Cecil Beaton, the most beautiful dining room in London. Unfortunately the famous Brasserie has now closed and a new owner has converted it into a "Cheers" bar. However, the Grill Room is still in business. With gilt edged mirrors, crystal and red velvet, it conjures up the Edwardian elegance with a French touch. Sir Herbert Tree once commented, "If you want to see English people at their most English, go to the Cafe Royal where they are trying their hardest to be French".

It was in the Brasserie that poets, painters, wits and eccentrics gathered. Here Oscar Wilde held court night after night arguing into the small hours with, among others, Aubrey Beardsley, Frank Harris and Bernard Shaw. In November 1922, the somewhat startling announcement was made that the Cafe Royal was to be pulled down and rebuilt. "They might as well have told us," wrote Y W H Crossland, "that the British Empire is to be pulled down and redecorated." Charles Forte bought the Cafe Royal in 1954 and refurbished and extended it into the eight-storey conference and banqueting facility that stands in Regent Street today. The Grill Room is a "must".

QUOTATIONS

"One cannot think well, love well, sleep well, if one has not dined well."
Virginia Woolf

"Only dull people are brilliant at breakfast."
Oscar Wilde, *An Ideal Husband*

"Those who do not enjoy eating seldom have much capacity for enjoyment of any sort."
Charles William Elliot, *A Happy Life*

"A good cook is like a sorcerer who dispenses happiness."
Elsa Schiaparelli

"No mean woman can cook well, for it calls for a light hand, a generous spirit and a large heart."
Paul Gauguin

"Every night should have its own menu."
Balzac

"Beware of young women who love neither wine nor truffles nor cheese nor music."
Colette

"I never worry about diets. The only carrots that interest me are the number you get in a diamond."
Mae West

"Making love without love is like trying to make a soufflé without eggs."
Simone Beck

"Every fruit has its secret."
D H Lawrence

"In water one sees one's own face, but in wine one beholds the heart of another."
French Proverb

18 St Paul's Church, Covent garden - the setting for the first scene of *My Fair Lady* (*right*)

19 The half-price ticket booth in Leicester Square (*below*)

20 Edmund Kean, in the foyer of the Theatre Royal (*left*)

21 St Paul's Churchyard, (*below right*)

22 David Garrick's house 27 Southampton Street (*below left*)

23 The National Portrait Gallery (*above right*)

24 Herbert Tree's plaque outside Her Majesty's Theatre (*right*)

25 Arthur Sullivan (of Gilbert & Sullivan); statue on the Embankment behind the Savoy Hotel (*above left*)

26 Dress Circle Shop, 57 Monmouth
Street (*opposite*)

27 The Savoy Hotel (*right*)

28 George Bernard Shaw's house,
Fitzroy Square (*below*)

29 St Paul's Church, known as the Actors' Church - some plaques (*above left*)

30 More plaques inside St Paul's (*above right*)

31 Henry Irving's statue next to the National Portrait Gallery (*left*)

32 Ad Lib restaurant (*opposite*)

33 Charlie Chaplin, Leicester Square (*left*)

34 Kettners Restaurant (*below*)

"There comes a time in every woman's life when the only thing that helps is a glass of champagne."

Bette Davis, *Old Acquaintance*

"We may live without friends, we may live without books, but civilized man cannot live without cooks."

Owen Meredith

"One should eat to live and not live to eat."

Molière, *L'Avare*

"Heaven sends us good meat, but the Devil sends cooks."

David Garrick

"That all softening, overpowering knell
The tocsin of the soul — the dinner bell."

Lord Byron

"Some day, you'll eat a pork chop, Joey, and then God help all women."

Mrs Patrick Campbell to Bernard Shaw

"This piece of cod passes all understanding."

Sir Edward Lutyens

"Fame is at best an unperforming cheat;
But 'tis substantial happiness to eat."

Alexander Pope

"There is no love sincerer than the love of food."

George Bernard Shaw

"At a dinner one should eat wisely but not too well, and talk well, but not too wisely."

Somerset Maugham

"The cook was a good cook, as cooks go, and as good cooks go, she went."

Saki

"Most dear actors, eat no onions or garlic, for we are to utter sweet breath."

Shakespeare, *A Midsummer Night's Dream*

CHAPTER NINE

THE THEATRE MUSEUM

The Theatre Museum in Covent Garden is one of the most interesting places to visit if you care deeply about the history of the British theatre and of all the performers, actor-managers, directors, costumiers and productions of the past few hundred years. It is packed with marvellous treasures, from a cape that Henry Irving wore, to a collection of paintings from the Villa Mauresque which were the private collection of Somerset Maugham. It is fascinating to see the old programmes, the playbills, the photographs, and, in a series of display cases, the costumes and belongings of theatrical legends.

The Theatre Museum also contains a wonderful research library where you can explore their files with a brilliant selection to choose from. There are letters and diaries of well-known historical figures, and all the records kept of performances and productions from Sheridan to Shaw.

Little did I know what my first visit would lead to. Walking through the galleries I admired the portraits of the famous actors and actresses of the past, the paintings sometimes depicting them playing the roles that immortalised them, others in costume for a new play or Shakespeare role. The thought occurred to me while studying the paintings, how interesting it would be to find out more about all these people and about their personal lives. Whom did Henry Irving marry? Whom did Ellen Terry marry? Did she give up the theatre for her family? Where did she live? Did Irving retire, or did he die still in costume? (He died in the lobby of a Bradford hotel after giving a performance of *The Bells* by Mathias, in the part he made famous.)

That evening, following my first visit, I began devising an anthology about the personal life of British theatre personalities and their families. After some further thought, I wrote to the Theatre Museum and sent them a proposal with regard to presenting the anthology in the small theatre there. I outlined the theme and suggested that perhaps some members of a theatrical dynasty might be persuaded to perform in it.

I contacted Corin Redgrave and Daniel Thorndike and invited them to read the script, but in addition asked them to read their favourite love poetry and talk a little about their families and tell some anecdotes about their illustrious predecessors. Dan and Corin were wonderful. He talked about Sybil Thorndike, Lewis Casson, and of his father, Russel Thorndike. Corin spoke about his grandfather, Roy Redgrave, who emigrated to Sydney, Australia and became a well-known star there. He even wrote his own epitaph to be published after his death — which appeared in the *Sydney Morning Herald*.

We first presented the show in the small theatre, then I began a series of Sunday afternoon performances in the Paintings Gallery. Each week we would have a visiting special guest. Corin asked his daughter, Jemma, and they did a show together with Tamsin Olivier, Lord Olivier's daughter. Some of the actors who had been in the Old Vic company on the Australian tour took part. Jimmy Ottaway was one. Each week we would alternate the verses and the anecdotes, depending on the personality we were featuring.

Many actors and actresses took part and we grew enough to take on a second venue, just around the corner in Bedford Street, for the Club for Acts and Actors. The script changed week to week and, when we decided to have some music included, we featured singers and pianists.

I called the show *Love from Shakespeare to Coward* and the script was devised from love poetry, verse, prose and anecdotes about the theatre.

It seemed to make the paintings and exhibits come alive especially when Dan Thorndike pulled out of his pocket a pair of gloves belonging to Henry Irving after he had just told us about his father meeting him years ago. Dan also told of his father's career and how he had participated in Sybil's first acting efforts, in the family home behind the drawn curtains of the living room. *The Dentist* was her first play, when she demanded that they "chop off his head" rather than extract the tooth.

We held showcases for recently graduated drama students as well. They would perform in the show and invite theatrical agents and managements to view their work. Each week whether it was at the Museum or the Club we would perform *Love*, and these students would take home with them the knowledge of their former theatrical "greats'" achievements.

Noel Coward's belongings are featured in a display case in one of the galleries — his dressing gown, cigarette case, photos, programmes and music, all of which bring back the glamour of those times. Julie Andrew's ball gown which she wore in *My Fair Lady* is in another space, the piano from *Salad Days* given by Julian Slade is there; all the exhibits are carefully labelled and well lit as you wander through a maze of corridors.

Love From Shakespeare To Coward has been running since 1992 and is still being performed in London and various venues. The King's Head

Theatre in May 1997 saw Judy Campbell and the American actress Kim Hunter perform it there and in 1997 the first performance in the States took place at the Columbia Artists' Association on West 57th Street, New York.

The Theatre Museum has a lively programme of events and play readings as well as receptions for theatrical personalities. Often London theatre critics and writers take part in seminars and workshops as well as lectures. Well known West End actors and actresses give talks and join in lively discussions.

Prepare to spend at least two hours to visit the Museum as there is so much to see and they now have video recordings you can watch from the Museum's own collection.

To visit the Library, it is necessary to phone in advance to make an appointment.

Don't forget to ask at the front desk for the month's events and what is happening in the Painting Gallery.

Extracts from *Love from Shakespeare to Coward*

ACT ONE

Actress

Romantic love, passionate love, theatre people's love for the theatre. Poets, playwrights and actors all experience the anguish of having to choose between their love of the theatre, and their love in their private lives.

Actor

Shakespeare's love for the theatre was so great that he left his wife and children in Stratford to make his way to London. He began writing plays, but was grief-stricken when his only son died at eleven.

Actress

Ellen Terry said: "My family means more to me than the theatre," and she worried about them during her long tours in America. She tried to ease her conscience by sending them large sums of money.

Actor

Noel Coward hated to fall in love. "It is too painful and too inconvenient." As the years slipped by, he wanted none of it.

Actress

It is interesting to speculate what Shakespeare would have thought of Noel Coward if they were to meet at the same age. Shakespeare must have been to a great number of "marvellous parties" and no doubt he would have enjoyed Coward's *Mad Dogs and Englishmen*. Shakespeare had the gift of rapier wit and sophistication, as did Coward. Coward's song, *If Love Were All*, would certainly have appeared cynical to the author of *Romeo and Juliet*. But first of all let us hear from Shakespeare. Here is Juliet waiting for her Romeo.

Actress 1

Gallop apace you fiery-footed steeds,
Towards Phoebus' lodging; such a waggoner
As Phaethon would whip you to the west,
And bring in cloudy night immediately.

Spread thy close curtain, love-performing night!
That runaway's eyes may wink, and Romeo
Leap to these arms, untalk'd of and unseen!
Lovers can see to do their amorous rites
By their own beauties; or, if love be blind,
It best agrees with night.

Come, civil night,
Thou sober-suited matron, all in black,
And learn me how to lose a winning match,
Played for a pair of stainless maidenhoods;
Hood my unmanned blood, bating in my cheeks,
With thy black mantle; till strange love, grown bold,
Think true love acted simple modesty.

Come, night! come, Romeo! come, thou day in night!
For thou wilt lie upon the wings of night,
Whiter than new snow on a raven's back.
Come, gentle night; come, loving, black-browed night,
Give me my Romeo : and, when he shall die,,
Take him and cut him out in little stars,
And he will make the face of heaven so fine
That all the world will be in love with night,
And pay no worship to the garish sun.

O! I have bought the mansion of a love,
But not possessed it, and, though I am sold,
Not yet enjoyed. So tedious is this day
As is the night before some festival
To an impatient child that hath new robes
And may not wear them.

Actor

Love comes in many guises. Jealousy and infidelity are two of them. Here is what Shakespeare wrote about infidelity; this is Emilia's speech from *Othello*.

Actress 1

But I do think it is their husbands' faults
If wives do fall. Say that they slack their duties,
And pour our treasures into foreign laps,
Or else break out in peevish jealousies,
Throwing restraint upon us; or say they strike us,
Or scant our former having in despite:

Why, we have galls; and though we have some grace,
Yet have we some revenge. Let husbands know
Their wives have sense like them. They see, and smell,
And have their palates both for sweet and sour,
As husbands have.

What is it that they do
When they change us for others? Is it sport?
I think it is. And doth affection breed it?
I think it doth. Is't frailty that thus errs?
It is so too.

And have not we affections,
Desires for sport, and frailty, as men have?
Then, let them use us well, else let them know
The ills we do, their ills instruct us so.

Queen Elizabeth I 1533 — 1603

England's "virgin queen", daughter of Henry VIII and Anne Boleyn, was well read in Latin, Greek, French and Italian, and translated works of ancient literature. Like any educated person of her day, she wrote poetry as a matter of course. She refused all offers of marriage, partly for political reasons (perhaps also because she loved Robert Dudley, Earl of Leicester who was already married). She was married to her kingdom, which she restored to stability and prosperity.

Queen Elizabeth never attended the Globe Theatre, but knew Shakespeare because she inherited the "King's Company" of actors of which he was a member. Here is one of her own poems:

Actress 1

Importune Me No More

When I was fair and young and favour graced me,
Of many was I sought their mistress for to be,
But I did scorn them all and answered them therefore,
Go, go, go, seek some other where,
Importune me no more

Actress 2

How many weeping eyes I made to pine with woe,
How many sighing hearts I have no skill to show,
Yet I the prouder grew, and answered them therefore,
Go, go, go, seek some other where,
Importune me no more.

Actress 3

Then spake fair Venus' son, that proud victorious boy,
And said, fine dame since that you have been so coy,
I will go pluck your plumes that you shall say no more,
Go, go, go, seek some other where,
Importune me no more.

Actress 4

When he had spake these words such change grew in my breast,
That neither day nor night since that I could take any rest,
Then lo, I did repent of that I said before,
Go, go, go, seek some other where,
Importune me no more.

Actor

Richard Burbage was born in 1567. He was one of Shakespeare's first interpreters, the original creator of *Hamlet, Othello* and *Lear*, and was one of the three fellow actors to whom Shakespeare left money in his will. He was so closely identified with Shakespeare's plays that people did not realise Shakespeare was dead until Burbage himself died too.

Here is a poem written by Austin Dobson called *When Burbage Played*.

Actor 1

When Burbage played, the stage was bare
Of fount and temple, tower and stair.
Two broadswords eked a battle out;
Two supers made a rabble rout;
The throne of Denmark was a chair!

Actor 2

And yet, no less the audience there
Thrilled through all the changes of despair,
Hope, Anger, Fear, Delight and Doubt,
When Burbage played.

Actor 3

This is the Actor's gift; to share
All moods, all passions, nor to care
One whit for scene, so he without
Can lead men's minds the roundabout,
Stirred as of old these hearers were
When Burbage played.

Actress

This is what William Hazlitt wrote on actors and acting:
    One of the most affecting things we know is to see a favourite actor take leave of the stage. We part with him as we should with one of our oldest and best friends. There is no class of society whom so many persons regard with affection as actors. We greet them on the stage; we like to meet them in the streets: they almost always recall to us pleasant associations; and we feel our gratitude excited, without the uneasiness of a sense of obligation. The very gaiety and popularity, however, which surrounds the life of a favourite performer, makes the retiring from it a very serious business.

Actress

And here is an anecdote about Burbage and Shakespeare that breathes life into them, recorded at the time by Francis Bacon:

Actor

Upon a time then Burbage played Richard III there was a citizen grew so far in liking with him that before she went from the play she appointed him to come that night unto her by the name of Richard the Third.

Shakespeare overhearing their conclusion went before, was entertained, and at his game 'ere Burbage came. Then message being brought that Richard the Third was at the door, Shakespeare caused return to be made that William the Conqueror was before Richard the Third.

Francis Bacon (1561 — 1626)

Actress

If an Actress falls in love with someone outside the theatre, can she be tempted to leave her career when he courts her with these words?

Actor 1

    Come live with me and be my love,
    And we will all the pleasures prove,
    That valleys, groves, hills and fields,
    Woods, or steepie mountain yields.

61

Actor 2

And we will sit upon the rocks,
Seeing the shepherds feed their flocks,
By shallow rivers, to whose falls,
Melodious birds sing madrigals.

Actor 3

And I will make thee beds of roses,
And a thousand fragrant posies,
A cap of flowers, and a kirtle,
Embroidered all with leaves of myrtle.

Actor 1

A gown made of the finest wool,
Which from our pretty lambs we pull,
Fur lined slippers for the cold;
With buckles of the finest gold.

Actor 2

A belt of straw, and ivy buds
With coral clasps and amber studs,
And if these pleasures may thee move,
Come live with me, and be my love.

Actor 3

The shepherds' swains shall dance and sing,
For thy delight each May morning,
If these delights the mind may move,
Come live with me and be my love.

Chapter Ten

Passionate Pilgrimages

Romantic love, passionate love, theatre people's love for the theatre. Poets, playwrights and actors all experience the anguish of having to choose between their love of the theatre, and their love in their private lives.

The second part of this book is not a theatre guide but rather a report on other things to do when you can't go to, or can't work in the theatre.

What do actors do when they can't get work in the theatre?

It may sound self indulgent to say there is a tremendous amount of anguish and torment. Simon Callow says in his marvellous book, *On Being An Actor*, that he nearly went mad when he was out of work. At one stage he says he was in a state of continuous turmoil, and if he hadn't found acting he might have gone insane.

Is it a disease? Or is it that you are born with a gene which makes you an actor? You are not really breathing unless you are doing it. I suppose actors, perhaps sometimes directors, certainly family members, understand the disease.

The general public see actors as colourful, charismatic creatures who may be rather immature in their need to work, but what they don't see is the despair, the turmoil, the doubts about whether to act at all, or their sometimes dismal private lives. Superstars' domestic life may be in the newspapers but not the seventy-eight per cent of the acting profession who live below the poverty line.

When I returned to London for the first time, after the Australian tour in mid-winter, I knew what Simon Callow meant. But besides the unemployment was the bitter weather and the frustrating round of agents — using your energy up and achieving nothing. It is a torment and these chapters are an account of some of the pilgrimages I took when there was no work and no sun. I felt if I was destined not to continue as an actress, then I had to travel. I wrote across my diary "Passionate Pilgrimages", and here are some of them.

The urge to make pilgrimages to places glorified by the heroes and heroines of our imagination is a deep one. What images would be conjured up by the town of Stratford-on-Avon if Shakespeare hadn't been born there? What is Athens, other than the home of the great playwrights of antiquity — Aeschylus, Sophocles, Euripides and Aristophanes; the writers

63

Plato, Aristotle and the philosophers? Travellers can go to places where characters, possibly entirely mythical, lived, such as Mycenae, Troy and closer to home, Baker Street.

Practical difficulties are no obstacle. The conquest of Palestine by the Arabs led to the First Crusade, which established a European kingdom there, to ensure the possibilities of pilgrimages to the Holy Land, and in spite of changes of government over the intervening centuries, pilgrimages still continue.

It is fortunately not quite so difficult in our time to make pilgrimages to the places which are the subject of the present book.

In the following chapters we will visit some of the homes of the celebrated including the Villa Mauresque, in the South of France, owned by Somerset Maugham, who is an inspiration to all struggling playwrights. Maugham wrote plays for ten years before he had his first produced. After his earlier struggles he gained fame as a writer of short stories and at one time had four plays running simultaneously in London's West End. His home for many years and where he died, was the Villa Mauresque on Cap Ferrat, one of the most beautiful places on the French Riviera.

Somerset Maugham wrote the novel, *The Razor's Edge*, which is a classic tale about one man's voyage to search for and find out for himself the meaning of life. When I first read the novel it had a profound impact on me and I was fascinated to follow his journey and motivations through the book. So I suppose my passionate pilgrimages are partly to assuage, or to discover the feelings of emotions that these artists' lives evoke. Obviously they had passions of their own, and they had their heroes, their ambitions, their goals. One wonders what motivated Maugham to write about the people he met during his world travels. Who were his heroes? And who were the heroes of Keats and Byron?

Sometimes, if you are extremely fortunate, by visiting a place you feel a sense of that person and know why they wrote, painted, composed or what they felt about their work.

The accounts of my grandfather's explorations in the mountains of Tasmania were horrendous — of battling against fierce, unexplored bush in tremendous storms, with tents and food being swept away in howling gales and no relief in sight for weeks. They made me realise just how primitive and difficult those ordeals must have been. Perhaps descendants of explorers, I thought, might inherit the genes of their ancestors, and the energy or motivation is born in you. I certainly thought that having hiked through many mountain ranges, later opened up by my father, stood me in good stead when exploring more civilised parts of the world. At least my grandfather had a mountain named after him in Tasmania which I suppose must have been worth the effort! Sharland's Peak lies south-west of Devonport in the north of the island.

There must have been a spiritual need to try to explore the Island, which is the same for some of the people who trek to the Himalayas and for the ones that reached the top of Mount Everest first.

The choices people make, when they have the opportunity to choose, reflects their personalities as well as their values. Some people choose to be limited by their occupations, their way of making money and spend their lives in the same place or country where they pursue this limited ambition. Others consider themselves citizens of the world; they consider nothing human as alien to them, and therefore feel that they are aliens nowhere.

They travel and explore. While there is little nowadays to explore in the sense of being first to see some part of the earth, there is the opportunity to live in other than one's native place. To do so requires a sense of adventure and the willingness to take risks, because every change is a risk. So that to choose change and the accompanying risk requires certain traits of character, some self confidence and some imagination. I am not talking about people who are forced to change countries by war, political or economic conditions — they are essentially refugees; they are driven rather than driving themselves, passive victims rather than active seekers of the strange, the exotic and the romantic.

Actually the urge to explore is innate; it can be seen in two- and three-year olds who "get into everything". Why they need to do so is primarily a matter of self-confidence, which is born from the absence of fearful experiences, and nurtured by success, which is the finding of pleasure in trying something new.

Travellers are like Cortez, the explorer, who first crossed the Isthmus of Panama, and "gazed at the Pacific with a wild surmise," as John Keats wrote, comparing his discovery to his own (less dangerous) discovery of Homer. But those who choose to go and live in a foreign country take risks that their more stay-at-home contemporaries avoid; they face indifference or antagonism, struggle with the different habits and customs of their new country, new language perhaps, and the loss of familiar friends and faces. As the risks are great, so are the rewards. There is the expanding of horizons both literal and metaphorical. One sees how other people, and therefore oneself, can live and one is thus able to think differently. One has something to take there as well, and so there is the possibility of living differently or "better", or with greater convenience than the "natives" do, and one can share this with them. There is also a sense of achievement in overcoming the various obstacles and the enjoyment of what the new country has to offer. It can some times lead to a wonderful contentment and happiness not found previously. So instead of buying a new car, or a new house, maybe try a new country for a while.

I called my unemployment the Lady Macbeth period. Speeches I was learning for an audition had to be repeated over and over again to get them into my head. After I had failed to get the part, I decided to leave London to escape the winter. But the speeches didn't go away. You learn them, repeat them like a robot, then you go on to other Shakespearean text because it is essential to keep it in your memory.

Practice, practice, practice. It was a kind of mantra. Certainly it helped to run through my speeches, poetry, anything to keep your lines alive. "To Be or Not to Be" was a favourite; also Viola's speeches from *Twelfth Night* — a joy to recite. Actors move their lips in the street; they mumble to themselves, they pull faces, and live in their own world for long periods of time.

The following chapters are about places of escape from the anguish and torment of being out of work. There will be no mention of the daily mumbles, only to say they were always present whether on board ship, or in Tangier or Jamaica. "To be or not to be" seemed to be more in my head for some reason in the last days in Tangier.

It was then I knew I wanted to spend more time at sea —now the time had come. I took a ship to Gibraltar.

When I left Hobart to study in London, I left by sea in a P & O ship which took twenty-eight days to reach England, via Colombo (Sri Lanka), Aden, the Red Sea, Port Said and the Suez Canal. In those days, even though there were no programmes for passengers, other than a violinist playing at afternoon tea, the experience of travelling by sea was enthralling; magical, romantic, and very exciting. For some reason, the passengers did all seem as if they were out of a Maugham or Coward short story and most of them had interesting lives and stories to relate.

These ships still retain these traditions, particularly on board the Queen Elizabeth II, where the ship's officers display such efficiency and confidence in the performance of their duties and in passenger contact that you feel as if you are stepping into a rather royal palace, where protocol and discipline are all part of life everywhere.

The first chapter is devoted to the lure of the big ships.

First of all, you call the QE II a "ship"! I am still amazed when talking to world travellers that they so often refer to these great ocean-going cruisers as "boats"; it is like calling a great restaurant a "cafe", or perhaps a Rolls Royce a jalopy. A boat is what goes on a ship. The QE II, especially, is a ship in every sense of the word. The pure majesty of her appearance is particularly stunning if you are approaching by foot the pier where she is anchored.

The bow is big, black and wonderful. The vessel is huge, and is seen to be so when one stands, for instance, on the pier. The immediate effect is to raise your spirits and quickly to make you feel the lure of far-away places. Suddenly you are transported from your immediate surroundings, almost disorienting your sense of time and place; it's like coming out of a cinema, and finding yourself in a completely new world. The horizon of your dreams is there before you. Unknown places, adventure, new sensations await, and for some people like me, a terrific sense of stimulation of the spirit. It never fails — leaving yesterday, leaving your present life, suddenly to board a vessel which is so large you can begin a new life immediately. Perhaps it is the instant remedy for boredom or a dull routine which is difficult to escape. Suddenly you are transported to a new environment, a new routine and quite possibly given a new lease on life.

My father once told me to watch for the "green flash" on the horizon at sunset; just as the sun sinks below the horizon, there is supposed to be a flash across the sea. I did once see it but his words always remind me how vulnerable we are to the force of nature.

Perhaps by coincidence, most of the people in this book enjoyed travelling by ship, and most of them sailed on the Queen Mary, or the first Queen Elizabeth. It also may be a matter of generation; being in Australia during the war and not ever dreaming that one day, we would travel overseas. The possibility was remote as nobody did go overseas except to fight.

Britain's island race with its tradition of "ruling the waves" through victories at sea refined the training of ship's officers in colleges and at sea to such an extent that the finished product turned out to be the most competent and knowledgeable men anywhere.

The mystique and magic of far-flung ports must appeal to all world travellers. In the early years of this century, the ships weren't as comfortable as they are now. There was no air-conditioning, for example, on my first P & O ship, so it was extremely hot in the cabin going through the tropics. Still, we were young and carefree and uncomplaining. Everything was a adventure with a capital A! The ports of call were not as commercialised as they are now, and each one offered some exotic hotel or sight-seeing tour which showed the natural beauty of the area. I don't know if the Mount Lavinia Hotel still exists in Sri Lanka, but in those days it was an old (not crowded with tourists) palatial hotel with an air of exotic elegance, similar to the Raffles Hotel in Singapore. Large ceiling fans and waving palm trees cooled the wide verandas where you sat drinking rum or gin slings and wearing your "whites", the perfumed air rivalling the best of Chanel.

It is hard to imagine how writers like Maugham and Coward found time to do any work at all while sailing in those waters as there was so much to see and so many people to meet. Coward's fame had already spread to the outer reaches of the British empire, so he was swept away by eager hostesses at every opportunity.

These were the days when men wore pith helmets and khaki on shore when the women were in light blue dresses such as seen in the film *A Jewel in the Crown*, and the sight of blue jeans everywhere had not invaded the sophisticated hotels of the colonies.

I travelled with a girlfriend from school. Not having experienced the various levels of sophistication which we found on board ship, we quickly learnt how to keep our mouths shut and just watch and listen. We made friends of the junior doctor on board and he was a great source of information about the ship's rules and regulations as well as filling us in about the types of passengers on board. He could tell at a glance, where people were from, where they were going and what nationality they were, without having even met them.

For the officers on board and the cruise staff, this was their entire world, They were there for the passengers and to see everybody had a memorable time. It is a "calling" for some, and many marriages have been broken because of the time spent at sea by a newly qualified officer. My cousin married one of the Chief Engineers on a P & O ship, and, after their first-born arrived, she found the loneliness without him too difficult, and he left his naval career because of it. It is almost impossible to have a happy marriage if you are married to a naval man, it seems. One has only to read about the Duchess of York, for example, to realise what the separation meant to her.

Most of the writers, performers and artists in the first part of this century, particularly before air travel was common between the British Isles and the United States, sailed on these ships, as readers of their biographies know. The photographs of the cabins, the public rooms and the parties on board are readily available as well as the passenger lists. All these people loved meeting their contemporaries. Often there were deals made on board and show business productions were created. Noel Coward wrote of how well he got to know Lord and Lady Mountbatten on one transatlantic crossing and how the idea for the film made by Coward based on Lord Mountbatten's ship was born (*In Which We Serve*).

Read a biography of Sir Noel Coward, anyone of them will mention his passion for the sea and for travelling by ship. He sailed frequently and often wrote about the joy and his love for ships. He composed many of his songs on his voyages and of course one of his most popular songs is *Sail Away*. "When the storm clouds are gathering…"

The times he wrote about were almost Edwardian in that everyone took great care to appear properly dressed at all times, and etiquette was very important on board — it still is.

It is impossible, when sailing on the QE II, not to be reminded of the creative people who travelled, sometimes working at their art on board, to the point of almost living in a dream world, as if the current life was not paradise enough. A voyage around the Mediterranean on the ship combines the luxury of a great hotel with the stimulus of fascinating ports of call, without the tedium and irritations of travel by land. The QE II is the last of the great ocean liners of the past and will almost certainly not be replaced when it is eventually phased out.

It is surprising then that it has featured in so little fiction compared to the Orient Express. It is for the duration of each voyage a miniature city, with its working population outnumbering the rich and the retired, all classes containing their hierarchies, vanities, and jealousies, thankfully without violence, poverty or the depressing presence of the homeless or poor. A novelist could first describe a typical day, beginning with breakfast in the cabin, making a leisurely progress through the activities of the day, the innumerable meals of varying complexity, the entertainment and games, the meetings and flirtations. As well there is the sense of something about to happen. But what?

Nothing sordid, like a commonplace murder or violent crime, but perhaps the disappearance of a priceless treasure, a work of art so well known as to be recognisable on sight. There should be on hand a world renowned solver of mysteries, a Hercule Poirot, and a variety of suspects, all of whom have good taste and intelligence. In the end, the puzzle would be solved, not by the famous sleuth, but a member of the crew (an officer, of course!).

Writers seem to love ship-board life. Often they can work in their cabins and socialise only when they feel like it. I now work for an agency which is about to hold an International Authors' Festival on board the Queen Elizabeth II, and for the past months we have been planning and inviting world-renowned authors to sail across the Atlantic and talk about their writing. It is quite possible you might meet your favourite author if you check the schedules and brochure this year. Arthur Hailey, Tom Keneally, Tom Clancy, Art Buchwald, Bill Bryson and many others will be sailing through 1998. George Plimpton, who started the Paris Review many years ago, has agreed to be the host for the 1998 Festival and he will be part of the world cruise as well.

We are hoping to invite Harold Pinter, his wife, Lady Antonia Fraser, Margaret Drabble and Michael Holroyd as well as P D James, Bill Styron and many others.

In 1996 I was asked to lecture on the ship after I had presented my anthology of verse, prose and anecdotes about British theatre personalities called *Love from Shakespeare to Coward* at the Theatre Museum in London, with Corin Redgrave and Daniel Thorndike. I repeated the anthology as well as lecturing on the differences between the Broadway theatre and the West End.

Another lecturer on the same Atlantic crossing was the late Jack Tinker, former theatre critic of the London newspaper, *The Daily Mail*. He took part in the reading of the anthology and it was the last time he was seen in public as he died a week later. He had read some Oscar Wilde, and was a riot when he read the old Billy Bennett song, *My Mother Doesn't Know I'm on the Stage*.

Travelling on the ship seemed to be some kind of landmark — or rather seamark — as I had always wanted to sail on Cunard's flagship. From my earliest years in Hobart, watching the great ships from my bedroom window sail up the Derwent river into the harbour, I dreamed of sailing away somewhere. In the 1960s I lived mostly in Canada, far away from the coastline; in the '70s it was Europe and the Bahamas; in the '80s theatre work in New York. So now at last it was back to the sea.

CHAPTER ELEVEN

GIBRALTAR AND TANGIER

All actors are to seem what they are not;
Which to perform, themselves must be forgot;
Their minds must lost in character be shown,
Nor once betray a passion of their own.

Trying to forget myself was easy, but in the matter of subduing a passion of my own, it was far more difficult. The mumblings continued and still there was no job in sight. That winter I found that my theatre contemporaries held on through rain, fog, depression and unemployment.

The daily grind of standing in icy winds for ages at bus stops until three buses arrived at once, or worse, the descent into the tube, where the smell of foul air, the filthy corridors, the litter, noise, vomit and urine-splashed walls was too much; the final indignity was the travel on the tube train itself, pushed into a mass of people, your face in someone's armpit, their boot on your toes, their foul breath making your stomach heave until at last you got out into the open air again, to meet the filthy rain and cold and see the homeless in the shabby streets.

Survival tactics' time was here. So many Australians at this stage of their careers, disheartened and chilled to the bone, just went home. I didn't have enough money to go home and somehow my pride would not allow me to write and ask my parents for the fare. I wanted to travel although I couldn't afford it. The closest place I could think of which would be warm was Gibraltar. I bought a ticket and had twelve pounds left in savings.

The charm of Gibraltar in those days was considerable. The tourists had not yet arrived. The curiosity for new places was almost as strong as the need or necessity for tramping around agents' offices in London. How many actors and actresses had given it all up and were now either in some far-flung place on the globe, perhaps running a bar or a hotel or perhaps closer to home in a safe little house running a business somewhere? The adrenaline and memories of the theatre faded dimly into the past either over a second gin and tonic or hot chocolate and the telly, closer to home.

After finding a cheap hotel, leaving my battered suitcase there, I started walking through the old town. Mumble, mumble. The sea air, the

71

Rock towering above, the mixture of British, Spanish and Arabic voices made the town seem colourfully exciting. What a wealth of material here, a wealth of wonderful characters to study. But my enthusiasm was mixed with a certain feeling of anxiety. There was no one to share the experience with and nobody knew I was here. I had enough money for two days at the hotel plus my return fare but I quickly realised that I wanted to stay much longer. I must find a job! Where? I had two days' expenses. Where? It was a Saturday afternoon, everything was closing up, shutters going up, the market was packing up. I walked on. Several people smiled at me. The place was so small they even recognised a new face. A young, dark, attractive British(?) woman coming from the market with two small children nodded and smiled.

I desperately wanted to stay here. The thought of going back to London in all that gloom with no work was horrifyingly present. I would *have* to. There was no way out. So I took a ship to get a small respite; who was I kidding? I knew no one. What did I think was going to happen? Someone was going to descend from the top of the Rock with a West End contract?

Perhaps I could teach? Yes, fine. Great. How could you find a teaching job in two days? I passed the old market square, now deserted, and walked up the road towards the Rock itself. My mind was filled with contradictions, two voices, me and myself, arguing with each other. No, you can't stay here, it is not a good career move...Oh, yes I can, it is called survival. I loved the place, the sun, the freedom, the feel of the place. Suddenly I came to a building with a small sign on the fence. It said "British School". I stopped and gave it some thought. Why not? Nothing ventured nothing gained.

I knocked on the door. No one home. I knocked again more loudly. Please let someone be there! The door opened…it was the caretaker. He told me no one was at the school on Saturdays, but I had only two days, so after some careful questioning he told me that the woman who ran the school lived in the old "tower" on the other side of the Rock. I thanked him and descended back into the town and started walking up the other side of the Rock until I came to the "old tower". It was an impressive building with a part of a house inside it. I rang the bell. A young girl came to the door and said she was the maid. She said the family were out but if I would like to wait she would bring me a cup of tea. It felt rather awkward waiting there but I accepted. I wondered what they would think, or how they would react to a perfect stranger waiting for them in their living room. For forty-five minutes there was total silence. I tried to ascertain who I was waiting for by the photographs on the mantelpiece and on the piano, but I needn't have worried.

It was the woman I had seen in the market. She swept in, a tiny brunette together with her husband and two children. She mentioned she had noticed me in the market square. We had another cup of tea, then I explained that I was looking for work. It didn't faze her at all. It turned out that she had been a ballet dancer in London, knew all the anguish that I was experiencing, and had given it all up to marry a Brit in Gibraltar. They had opened the tiny school mainly to teach dancing, also to give music lessons for the local inhabitants. She asked if I played the piano — I told her I was a graduate from the Guildhall so she offered me the job of pianist for several ballet classes at the school —it was a start.

They invited me to stay on for dinner, then suddenly in came a Scottish chap in his seventies named Jock. Dear Jock — any Brit who lived on the Rock in those days will remember him. He ran the Toc H club in an old fort in the town, housing students who helped out with the day-to-day chores, as in a youth hostel, for their keep. He asked where I was staying and when I told him he immediately said, "You can't afford to stay there." So, after dinner, we drove down to the hotel, picked up my suitcase and I was given a room in the old fort! It overlooked the harbour, and when I had unpacked my few things, met the other students around the communal outdoor fireplace there, we listened to one of them play his guitar in the warm evening firelight.

The next day Jock said he had to make a day-trip for supplies across to Tangier in Morocco on the ferry and maybe I'd like to go with him. Why not? A few hours on the ferry and a chance to see the casbah in Tangier. He had friends over there who could probably help find me a full-time job for the winter which would pay more than playing for ballet classes a few hours a week. I said goodbye to my new-found friends and took the ferry.

Tangier was still an international zone. So the city was divided into Spanish, Arab, British and French zones. It was a cacophony of musical accents, costumes, customs, colourful scenes, tremendous energy and sexual excitement. I met many incredibly weird, bizarre and uninhibited people. The first day Jock and I spent there was a whirlwind one. He knew many people but he focused on the ones he knew who could help me. First we went to the American school; we had coffee with the principal, we talked for thirty minutes, then he offered me a job as a part-time primary teacher. The day was so eventful that I forgot about my past life. the theatre, the Guildhall, it was as if I was in another world. I was a student again, vividly trying to remember the sights and sounds as we sped through the town nearly knocking down the stalls on the footpath, rushing past Arabs in veils, fat jewelled ladies and carpet-sellers. I wouldn't have been surprised if we'd whizzed past Rick's Cafe and seen Bogart standing by the front door. There was a heavy perfume in the air, the pungent perfume that I recognised as Tangier.

Next stop was the American Embassy where we were shown in to see the Political Attaché, Robert Whittinghill. Whittinghill was the first American I had met in a working environment. He radiated warmth, wit and good health. He was impeccably dressed, charming, brief; he seemed to conjure up an image of polished efficiency and got straight to the point. I now had a job at the American school; where would I live? he asked. He and his wife had a new-born son and they were looking for a part-time nanny; I could have a suite of rooms in their mansion which was located next door to the Sultan's Palace, in return for some baby-sitting. He told us to meet him there in two hours, then he'd drive us up to the house.

Back down to the Arab quarter where we stopped for lunch. My first couscous and some raw Moroccan red wine. People came up to greet Jock and more friendships were made. Two hours later we were back at the Embassy and once again we were on wheels, speeding through the town. Everyone drove at breakneck speed. Up through the French quarter, I glimpsed designer clothes and perfume bottles in shop windows until suddenly we were high on a cliff, overlooking the straits of Gibraltar and the Atlantic Ocean. It was a breath-taking view with a refreshing light breeze cooling the three of us in the car. We turned and drove through double wrought-iron gates up to an impressive white marble, palatial home. Once inside, I was totally dumb-struck: pure white marble everywhere, exquisite Persian rugs on the floor, expensive antique furniture. Several servants bowed as we walked out to a large patio overlooking the ocean. It was then that I felt slightly shabby in my Marks and Spencer sweater and skirt — it should have been a white silk suit! It was like being on a set for a Noel Coward play while we waited for Mrs Whittinghill. They had been in Morocco for a year but surprise! She had been an actress on Broadway before her marriage. They took me up a flight of marble steps to show me the suite of rooms. The sitting room had a balcony overlooking the sea and they wanted to know if it would suit! The arrangements were quickly made. Three evenings a week I would baby-sit plus the weekends. A driver would take me to the school each day and I could come and go as I pleased. The baby was brought in and seemed to be adorable — he was. All I needed was to collect my belongings.

Before we caught the ferry back to Gibraltar, Jock suggested a drink at the Velasquez Hotel. The bar was on the top floor of the hotel; the sensational feeling of sophistication is still vivid in my memory. Some immediate reactions to places stay with you for the rest of your life. I had hardly ever been in a cocktail bar during my student days in London, it was just not on one's agenda. So the first view from this bar in Tangier was impressive. Totally glassed in, it had a soft blue tint around the windows; at night, the blue was picked up by concealed lights overhead, you looked out on the city and the water through a blue-green glow.

Everything was glass, chrome, white and crystal. It reeked of class. Again, a perfect Coward set. The Hollywood movies we watched as kids at Saturday matinees were immediately conjured up...here they were living in the flesh. Was that Barbara Hutton sitting over there?

If Ginger Rogers or Fred Astaire had walked in I wouldn't have been surprised.

Jock was drinking something red with a slice of orange in it. He suggested I have one too. My first Campari; I felt I really had begun to live in my own play. I noticed a white piano by the door, so as there were only two other people in the bar, I went over to inspect it. The barman asked if I would play something, so I did.

Half an hour later, one of the two people sitting by the window came over and introduced himself as the manager. They wanted a pianist for the cocktail hour. The thought of coming to this elegant bar again seemed miraculous. I explained I would be teaching and then baby-sitting. However, after discussing the matter the following week with the Whittinghills, we arranged that I could play there in the early evenings, after school from five to seven pm. It was finalised.

In those days, as in anyone's youth, you didn't worry where the next meal was coming from, or if you were dressed in the appropriate clothes, if you had or had not brought your toothbrush, if your bowels moved or not, or if your waistline had expanded; your aim was to gather as many new experiences as possible. I felt like Michael Palin. All I needed was some new clothes.

I stayed with Jock for a few more days helping to give the old Fort a really good spring cleaning as well as doing mounds of laundry. I felt I owed it to him for all his efforts on my behalf. Then I was back on the ferry to Tangier. I started teaching ten-year olds, mostly Moroccan boys who were street smart and quick as foxes. They kept knives in their desks to play with at recess time. Their names were incomprehensible and unpronounceable which didn't make this teacher the necessary voice of authority; that was unsettling to say the least. And I was outnumbered. However after I'd taken all their weapons away, and they only had the ammunition that they carried in their voices, I fared better. They soon learnt what detention and writing a thousand sentences after school meant. Astonished faces stared at me when I first ordered this punishment which they'd never heard of. Being a nanny and playing the piano at the Velasquez were far easier tasks.

Life up at the cliff-top mansion was a unique experience. The Whittinghills entertained lavishly. It was the first time I had experienced American hospitality. I was included in all their soirées. Some were business affairs when the guests spoke in French, Spanish or English; sometimes all three. Often there would be entertainment after dinner. Flamenco dancers would come up from one of the harbour-front cafes bringing their musicians with them. They'd dance dramatically while we all sat around in a circle clapping our hands in time to the guitars. Other evenings, we'd all drive down to one of the cafes to watch them in action there. In those days, the cafes were full of the local inhabitants, hardly any tourists at all, but I'm sure all this has changed now with the influx of cruise ships. Quite probably those old cafes are long gone or otherwise turned into expensive tourist traps.

During this time I got to know a few ruthless people, smugglers, drug-pushers and a woman who was trying to set up a phoney weight-loss clinic. I observed the types that hung out in the casbah and became paranoid when I was told about girls who were drugged, kidnapped and sold to the white slave trade. Then suddenly one day, amidst all the decadence and debauchery of the artistic community, I was introduced to a British titled lady who was one of the world leaders of the Moral Rearmament group.

She invited me for afternoon tea in her gracious drawing-room. The contrast was startling. As we sipped tea, she suggested I join the group and become an actress in their season of plays at the Westminster Theatre in London. Just as she was curious about my existence in Tangier, I was equally puzzled as to why she was living there. Her home, full of English furniture, was in stark contrast to the rest of Tangier. After another cup of tea, my curiosity was still not assuaged; I left her saying I would think about it. I never did find out why she lived in Tangier.

During the sea voyage back to England from Australia, I met and fell in love with the ship's junior surgeon. It was a twenty-three day voyage so we had plenty of time to get to know each other. He had just qualified to be a doctor in Dublin and was taking a break as a doctor at sea before starting up a practice. We went ashore together at the ports of call, spent hours of our time over dinner or a glass of wine, discussing our ambitions and hopes. I quickly realised his profession seemed far more intelligent than mine. Every actor has tremendous doubts from time to time about their careers. Being superficial and egomaniac were just some of the fears, as well as the all too real unemployment. After arrival back in the UK, he went off to work in Wales, to a mining village, while I did the rounds of the agents once more in London. It was on one freezing cold night, still unsure of marriage that I decided I had to go off somewhere again to think things over.

Aware of life moving on, other actresses either playing something marvellous on stage or miserably out of work, I knew this was a turning point.

I suppose that when you are in love the aims you have are often sublimated to the aims of the other person. Yes, perhaps it was a rationalisation, but after waiting for him one evening in the emergency room of the hospital, I realised the drama I was seeing there was more intense and life-shattering than playing Lady Macbeth on stage. It was totally and immediately all-consuming. I wondered if all actors, given the chance of suddenly becoming a surgeon and saving someone's life, would put an end to their character creations? Was all this totally naive? Probably. You do what you have to do. Circumstances, opportunities, luck still do count in an acting career. Being at the right place at the right time is part of the fate which hangs in the balance. Ask any actor.

Chapter Twelve

Noel Coward's House in Jamaica

Midwinter in London. Freezing cold, icy winds, incessant rain, dark miserable afternoons, wet Sundays, sagging spirits and dull despair.

It was around that time I became immersed in Noel Coward's autobiography. It really became a kind of life-saver — a book I read over and over again because not only was it enjoyable but it was a fantastic escape. Other theatrical personalities were written about of course, but none so glamorous.

It was the style of his life which was so impressive. He left London, even though in his day I'm sure it was not as dirty or litter-filled, first living in the country and then travelling all over the world.

Many other writers and actors did this of course but not with the same kind of glamour. He seemed to put each place on the map, a trend-setter before the name was even invented.

He moved to Bermuda and the islanders are still proud to show off the house which he bought there. Later on he made Jamaica his home, and each night as I lay in bed in London listening to the rain, wind, thunder and traffic noises, I'd visualise the life I was reading about. What impressed me a great deal was the fact that Coward could afford to pay and keep his companions. To have a live-in secretary to answer letters, pay bills and arrange the housekeeping seemed the extreme of luxury, as did the ability to discuss his daily writing with them, and sometimes to receive inspiration from them. They were his support system.

Coward seemed unique in his writing for the theatre because his work somehow hinted at international travel and glamour. He wrote a novel about an imaginary tropical island, and painted canvases, not of London or of cities, but of wild tropical places — beaches, natives, palm trees and exotic scenes which he had grown to love. He loved Jamaica and it is astonishing that he managed to write, paint and compose there in the heat with all the distractions of a fabulous view of mountains, oceans and wild life from his patio study. Even Somerset Maugham, who had from his study window a view of the coastline of the Côte d'Azur, boarded up that window as he found the view too distracting. But the lives that these two writers lived was incredible. They partied, travelled, bought and sold houses, journeyed across oceans and met influential people

78

everywhere they went. Coward described their arrival in Rio where they were wined and dined every night and were invited to more social events than they cared to attend.

The more I read about their active careers, the more I receded down into my blankets, astonished and impressed that they achieved all that they did. They seemed to have lived on a different planet. Coward was not a rich man so it was even more bewildering that he managed to do it all. At one time, before he was fifty, he owned a country house with a tennis court and a huge garden in Kent, three houses in St Margaret's Bay, a town house in London and then his house in Jamaica. He also bought an apartment in New York after selling his house in Bermuda. In his autobiography he mentions that he was attracted to perform in Las Vegas only because he had nothing in the bank. And yet he believed he was not an extravagant man.

All this affected me greatly. What was I doing, trying to write plays and sending them to fringe theatres in London, surviving the tube journeys by day and reading about Coward by night?

I wrote a play called *Jamaican Interlude* to try and capture some of the frustration of not being able to travel or live there. The story was about a group of people who are staying in a hotel in Jamaica near "Firefly", the home of Coward. Then it had just been renovated by Chris Blackwell and opened to the public. Each hotel guest had come to visit Firefly, and in my play, I wrote the reasons why they had come. Rachel Kempson (Lady Redgrave) agreed to do a rehearsed reading of the play. She had known Coward well and in her book, *Life among the Redgraves*, she writes about the incident when her husband Michael spent the night with Coward before going off to the war, rather than with her.

The play was narrated at the piano by Bruce Ogston, a pianist/singer who specialises in Coward's songs. He played the hotel pianist and each scene was preceded by a Coward song. Bruce was the pianist at The Ivy for many years. Unfortunately no producers were available to come to the reading, even though Rachel was making a rare appearance in London. Obviously I had dreams of it being snapped up as a T V movie or feature, filmed in Jamaica and featuring Firefly! I also hoped to interest Graham Payn who knew so much about his life, but he was working on his own book about him. I wanted to meet witty, intelligent, cultivated people interested in the arts, people as I imagined Coward to have been.

How you remember far-flung places always depends, I suppose, on your experiences there. If you are lonely or bored or the weather is bad, nothing is more depressing. In Somerset Maugham's short story, *The Book Bag*, he describes a traveller taking all his favourite books with him whenever he left home. That is one solution if you don't meet interesting people or if you are kept indoors by bad weather, I suppose. I began to travel with Sheridan Morley's book about Noel Coward. It became wine-stained and dog-eared, but no matter what the setting, whether a tediously long wait in an airport or eating alone in a strange restaurant, you could always imagine for amusement what Coward would have done under these conditions.

He had some disastrous holidays himself, as he has written, ranging from renting a boat which sank in a storm, to being holed up with flu in a Shanghai hotel. One wonders what books he travelled with on his journeys. He re-read most of his favourite writers over and over again. On his bedside the morning he died in Jamaica was a copy of a book by E Nesbit who was one of his best-loved authors.

Quite often, new thoughts arrest you in such places and whole areas of your life, not consciously worried about, rise to the surface, which probably would not have happened if you stayed at home. One could call them middle-of-the-night anxieties. I remember writing a letter in a hotel room in Nassau in the Bahamas, in the middle of the day as it happened, and I got up to look out the window and saw all the people sunning themselves on the brilliantly white beach below. The water was transparently green and breathtakingly beautiful. They were all having a great time sipping rum punches and diving into the sea. I suddenly thought that even if I started now, I could never become a novelist. A black cloud of depression descended; where the hell did that come from? I'd never tried to become a novelist, so why the anguish? The mood wouldn't lift. Suddenly I couldn't imagine how George Sand had written over a hundred novels. She also wrote plays, I reflected, and looked after Chopin at the same time. This mood continued until I spied a mouse running across the carpet (this was supposed to be a luxury hotel), so that made me exit rather quickly and go for a walk, thus dispelling the mood with a gloomy acceptance of my shortcomings as a writer.

Simon Callow's account of his stay on an island off Tahiti brilliantly evoked the feeling of wretchedness, even though he was suffering physically as well. I longed to hear some tropical stories which perhaps would inspire me to write a novel, even a short story. The only one which came immediately to mind was about a well-known figure in Nassau, but I felt sure I would have been sued if I wrote the story.

Even after years of rationalising the reasons why you keep putting up with winter, most people console themselves with memories of sunnier times and places. I began to plan another escape. You can't keep working artistically if you are freezing cold and miserable. Oh yes you can, I hear Simon Callow saying. I tried to write, I painted Australian landscapes; the whole day was spent trying to stay in contact with people who were working in the theatre. Reading biographies became a passion. Linking up the theatre personalities who worked together in London in the '20s and '30s proved to be a kind of tranquilliser. Successful, enthusiastic, stylish, well-connected, talented, they seemed to lead charmed lives.

Coward was my favourite. I re-read Cole Lesley's biography of him, *London, Switzerland, Bermuda and Jamaica.* My curiosity was about where he lived and how he lived grew to such intensity. I knew I had to do something about it.

The following winter I took a charter to Florida. While there I noticed that there was a special sailing at reduced prices on a ship which was stopping in Jamaica at Ochos Rios. I took it. There were three ports of call, and the cruise director was selling shore excursions to various beaches, and various bus tours. I asked him to announce that if there were any interested parties, a visit to Noel Coward's house in Port Maria could be arranged. There was absolutely no response at all. However a couple sitting at our dining table showed some interest as they didn't want to go on a bus tour. I knew the house was about twenty miles away so that the cost of a taxi would be rather high and the security would be risky with just the two of us. So I really enthused about it all, and they agreed to accompany us.

Next morning after the ship had berthed, we set off in a taxi decorated with a crucifix, baby slippers hanging from the rear-view mirror and a very talkative Jamaican driver whom we couldn't understand at all. He drove like a bat out of hell. The road was crowded with native children and animals walking up and down on either side. After we passed Ian Fleming's house, "Goldeneye", the road became even narrower. I remember reading the accounts of the partying that went on between Coward's house in Blue Harbour and Goldeneye. Jugs of martinis were consumed as they commuted between each other's beach-front homes with many celebrated guests accompanying them. Nearly everyone was a household name, from the Oliviers, to Joan Sutherland, Clifton Webb, Maggie Smith. In an account of Ian Fleming's wedding in Port Maria, the wedding party all drove back to Goldeneye for a wild celebration and it boggles the mind to think of them careering along this same road; it would have been almost as bad as driving intoxicated along the Amalfi coast road.

Finally we reached the road up to Firefly. It is still a dirt track, really more suitable for a jeep. How the Queen Mother's car managed it when she arrived to lunch with Coward is astonishing.

After paying a rather stiff admission charge and seeing the rising cost on the taxi meter, I think our dinner companions expected to see a mansion. They probably assumed that as Coward had been so famous, he would have had a luxurious villa. Coward had deliberately built a simple one-bedroom house, which was little more than a cottage, a simple kitchen leading to the living room and a veranda upstairs. Their first words were: "Is this it? Is this where he lived?" Of course I was absolutely fascinated by his small studio and patio where he worked. We were shown around by a guide who probably had never read any of Coward's work.

When we walked down to his grave, a short way from the house, the view was breath-takingly beautiful. I stood there imagining Coward's cocktail hour, then he and his friends would come here and watch the fireflies come out. The guide disappeared into a nearby hut which had been made into a souvenir shop, turned on a radio, and we suddenly were greeted with Julie Andrews singing *These Are a Few of My Favourite Things* very loudly. The atmosphere was totally lost through the incongruity of the whole thing. Fortunately we were the only people there that morning, so I managed to slip back into the house alone and spend some minutes in silence in those rooms, imagining how many marvellous parties must have been held there. His two pianos, side by side, are still there although in bad repair and some of his furniture and paintings still remain. We drove back to the ship in silence except for the driver who saved the day by recounting his life every time he had to stop at a traffic light. Back to the ship, and a week later I was back to the gloom of winter in England. Jamaica seemed, and was, a long way away.

CHAPTER THIRTEEN

SOMERSET MAUGHAM'S VILLA IN FRANCE

Cap St Jean Ferrat, France

Maugham was born in the British embassy in Paris, to which his father was legal consultant. For the first nine years of his life, Maugham spoke only French, and for the rest of his life was as much at home in France as in England, although his writings and the biographies about him mention few French friends or acquaintances. It is tempting to compare his mastery of English and indeed his style to that of Joseph Conrad whose native language was Polish. Maugham also was fairly fluent in German and less so in Spanish and Italian, and it is interesting that in his *Summing Up* he declared that there was no particular merit in learning foreign languages, except French. When working as a British spy in Russia during the First World War, he was hindered by his limited capacity in the Russian language.

His mother, to whom he was very close, died when he was nine years old, and his father two years later. He was then taken care of by a clergyman and his wife, and was an unhappy, shy child with a stammer which made him the butt of his schoolmates. He became a medical student and qualified as a doctor, though he never practised. However he believed that the experience was useful to him as a writer, giving him a knowledge of the lives of the poor, and a training in scientific method and logical thinking.

He was never poor himself. He inherited a modest income, which enabled him to mix with people much richer than himself; he was quite sociable and indeed fun-loving as a young man, but always conscious of the importance of money as a means to independence and the procurement of the more enjoyable things of life. His early adult live was a continual struggle. He wanted to be a writer, and wrote plays and novels but had continuing difficulties with publishers and agents. It was not until he was in his early thirties that he began to achieve fame and fortune with the production of his play, *Lady Frederic*. From that point on, his career was in the ascendant; he wrote play after play; at one point four of his plays were running simultaneously in the West End of London. He entrusted his savings to a good friend, Alanson, who invested them wisely and avoided losses during the 1929 stock market crash. Maugham said once that he had entrusted fifteen thousand pounds to Alanson, and some years later, realised he had become a millionaire. He was lionised both in England and the United States. He used his wealth to travel; he was an adventurous traveller, using his experiences as material for his books. He was particularly interested in the Far East, and took some hazardous voyages there during one of which he was nearly drowned. He also contracted malaria, which plagued him intermittently, and almost killed him. However his keen observation of British people living in the Far East and on the Pacific islands were the basis of many of his stories and plays, notably *Rain*. He continued to travel to the Far East into old age, but with diminishing returns in terms of written and published stories; in fact his last trip resulted in nothing at all. He found the people he met less interesting, but it may be that his increasing preoccupation with himself, his ideas, philosophy and health progressively diminished his curiosity about others' lives and experiences to the point that they did not seem to him worth writing about.

The house that he is most associated with of course is the Villa Mauresque which he bought in 1926. He immediately employed two architects to renovate it; the renovations took more than a year to finish, but he finally moved in the following year, in August 1927. It was his home for the rest of his life, except during the war years, when it was occupied by the enemy and virtually vandalised. However he had it cleaned up after the war, and his furniture and pictures, which had been given over to friends for safe-keeping, were returned. During all the years from 1927 onwards, he was seldom alone there; for a man who was reputed to be shy and diffident, it is remarkable that he had so many guests to what became a continual house party. His friends and guests included rich and titled people as well as those celebrated for artistic and literary achievement; Noel Coward, Hugh Walpole, Godfrey Winn, Beverley Nichols as well as Pablo Picasso and other artists. His family were frequent guests including Syrie, his wife, his daughter Liza and her husbands, Paravicini and later Lord John Hope, his brother, the Lord Chancellor of England, of whose career he was extremely proud, and his nephew Robin Maugham.

On Gerald Haxton's death, Alan Searle, his companion for thirty years, and his amanuensis, was left his estate. In his will he left the Villa Mauresque to Alan Searle, whom he had adopted, although the adoption was later annulled by the French courts, at the instigation of Maugham's daughter Liza. Almost as soon as he had inherited it, Searle sold the Villa Mauresque and the surrounding grounds to a developer. However the

35 Shaw's house, Fitzroy Square was also home to Virginia Woolf - see the plaque (*above left*)

36 David Drummond's shop in Cecil Court (*above right*)

37 This sign in Villiers Street marks where the Players' Theatre is underneath the arches of Charing Cross Railway (*below right*)

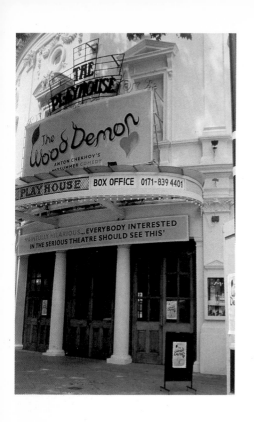

38 The Grill Room at the Cafe Royal, frequented by Oscar Wilde, Aubrey Beardsley,
Bernard Shaw and many celebrated writers, artists and actors (*above*)

39 The Grill Room - a detail (*opposite, left*)

40 The Playhouse Theatre - George Bernard Shaw's first play was produced here
(*opposite, far left*)

41 Samuel French's Theatre Shop, Fitzroy Street (*opposite, below*)

42 Royal Academy of Dramatic Art (RADA) (*above left*)

43 Ivor Novello's home in the Aldwych (*below left*)

44 The Sherlock Holmes Pub (*below right*)

45 The pub sign with Dr Watson on the reverse side (*opposite above*)

46 The Haymarket Theatre (*opposite below*)

47 John Gielgud, Emma Thompson and author (*opposite above*)

48 Harold Pinter, author, Lady Antonia Frazer (*opposite below*)

49 Firefly, Coward's home in Jamaica (*above right*)

50 Corin and Jemma Redgrave, and Lord Olivier's daughter, Tamsin, with the author (*below*)

51 Zeffirelli, Italian film and opera director / designer

Villa stands as a place of pilgrimage to those whose lives were affected in one way or another by his work.

I discovered his short stories and novels before the plays. He was a writer like Coward, who escaped the tedium of London life and even though he was passionate about the theatre, he wrote about the romance of travelling. His stories evoke the excitement of a world then far away, where people lived strange lives, sophisticated or simple; these characters are unforgettable. His cynicism and knowledge of human nature sometimes leaves one shocked and depressed, but he never fails to move you. The tales of the British overseas, ship-board companions or, reading between the lines, his own experiences are fascinating. He was an explorer, not of geographic areas, but of how people coped who lived overseas.

Perhaps back-packers these days don't have the opportunity to move in the circles he did when travelling, so it is an interesting history of what it was like to see strange lands before the days of mass travel.

He represented the unobtainable world of high society and wealthy connections; it was his creative drive that made him write about it.

I suppose I wanted to see where this man who had lived such a glamorous, adventurous life had finally chosen a house in which to settle down and continue his writing.

Impressive wrought-iron gates between the stone pillars, one of which has Maugham's well-known insignia inscribed on it, open into a flower-covered driveway which curves its way up to the villa which is hidden from the road. On your right you pass by the tree-lined tennis court which Maugham had built for his visiting house guests.

The villa itself, although it seems enormous from the driveway, is not that large inside. The architecture is Moorish and the inner courtyard gives the feeling of graciousness and airiness. Walking through the main rooms on the ground floor, you come out onto a large patio and swimming pool. The main bedrooms are on the first floor with a corridor looking out onto the courtyard. On the third floor was Maugham's study where he had blocked out the view from the window so he could work without distraction. His wonderful art collection given to the Royal National Theatre is now on view at the Theatre Museum in Covent Garden.

Just down the road, in this exquisitely beautiful part of the world is the famous Hotel du Cap where Maugham was a frequent visitor. It is worth a visit alone to have a drink on the terrace, or for the more adventurous to take the cable car, situated at the bottom of the garden, to the Beach Club below. There is a path winding around the pine trees and rocks at the water's edge which provides a delightful scenic walk to soak up the atmosphere and spirit of Cap St Jean Ferrat.

CHAPTER FOURTEEN

PUCCINI'S HOUSE IN ITALY

The House at Torre Del Lago

In 1894 Puccini discovered Torre del Lago, a little inland, but on the side of a lake. He bought the villa, and while he was living there he composed *La Bohème* which had its premiere in 1896, and subsequently *Tosca*, which premiered in 1900 in Rome.

His villa is worth a pilgrimage. Imagine the undistinguished town, a nondescript road leading to the edge of the lake, where the villa stands. As we were driving through the town which seemed deserted, I began having doubts as to my decision to find the villa. We had turned off the main motorway, the express route to the south, miles back and all seemed to be very flat and uninteresting. No dramatic scenery, just a very ordinary Italian suburb with overhead tram lines, lots of transport trucks and bicycles everywhere. We turned left along the lake road and there was the villa standing back slightly from the main road — a plain stucco house overlooking the lake. Fortunately it was open.

The front door leads directly into a small entrance area, then straight into the parlour. There was Puccini's upright piano against the left wall with the small table at the end of the keyboard with a lamp over it. It was here he did his composing, next to the piano or on the piano stool itself. Simple enough but somehow impressive. This was his home until 1921 when he had a villa built at Viarreggio, then moved there; however he never sold the villa at Torre del Lago; he returned occasionally to pursue his favourite recreation, shooing wildlife on the lake. The move was necessitated by the construction of a peat factory, the fumes and noise of which drove Puccini to relocate.

Puccini was buried in a tomb inside the villa at Torre del Lago. It seems rather strange to pass by him there when all around is the furniture and everyday articles he used. There are many photos on the walls; outside in a small pavilion is a rare collection of some of his manuscripts, letters, and memorabilia. His last year was spent in severe pain and when diagnosed with throat cancer, the doctors began slowly killing him by placing needles in his throat to try to cure the cancer until the pain caused him to have a heart attack which resulted in his subsequent death. It is difficult to imagine what agony he must have experienced and one wonders why such a genius was subject to so much horrific pain.

Torre del Lago is the principal remaining shrine and each year there is a small festival of his operas held in the open air. How, one wonders, could such dramatic works as *Tosca* and *La Bohème* been composed here? Puccini of course was himself a very emotional man, forced to leave his native Lucca (the nearby city where he was born) because of his seduction of Elvira; she was a married woman with whom he lived out his extraordinarily productive life, marrying her after the death of her husband. His music is about passion, and death, which he portrays as its inevitable result. His characters cannot and do not choose to do other than to live ruled by their instinctive desires, and if death results, they choose it only too willingly. His music soars and carries all before it; the unforgettable melodies and harmonies in his unique style crystallise a longing for the beloved which transcends the scandal and sheer horror of death and destruction. His characters are heroes and heroines of love, heroic because they dare all, risk all, lose all and are doomed.

How is it that his music conveys so much? Admittedly the association of ideas derives partly from the librettos, and Puccini himself was very aware of the importance of a good libretto, and much of his correspondence over the period in question is about these matters. But the music itself stands apart, haunting, creating indelible impressions of fear and longing. It does not suffice to analyse it technically — successions of chords, repetitions of themes, and so forth. There is the unique inspiration of genius itself, a genius which owes little to copying others, obviously the case because of Puccini's individual and unmistakable style.

Individual style was of course nothing new. Purcell, Handel, Mozart, all in the preceding century, had their own clearly recognisable styles in the shared manner of eighteenth century music; Puccini however has a more transparently personal style. One can tell little about Handel or what he felt about anything from his music, except that he wrote well to please the musically sophisticated audience of his time. But Puccini is different; his music reflects him more directly; one grasps that the intense feeling expresses what he himself experienced. Perhaps that is why those who visit Torre del Lago are in a way revealing themselves as people who attach importance to passion in its most unequivocal form. Such attitudes have little to do with art or an appreciation of it; it has to do with their basic feelings of romance and how these feelings have been stimulated and encouraged by Puccini's music — they probably know little of his life.

While music is both a craft and an art, like any professional, Puccini was so thoroughly enmeshed in the creation of music that the craft and the artfulness disappear, even if such skills were consciously invoked when he wrote his great operas. The librettos remain important; we know who wrote them, we know the stories from which they were derived, and we know what importance he attached to them.

A novel is one thing, an opera derived from it is such a totally different creation that they are practically unrelated experiences.

Read *La Dame aux Camelias* by Dumas, and then go to see *La Traviata*. Similarly, one can read a guide book about the Torre del Lago area and have no conception of what it feels like to go there and be in the surroundings and the very house where Puccini wrote the famous operas.

To visit Torre del Lago is not merely being transported a hundred years back, it is for the imaginative and romantic soul, being lifted into an eternal world where love and passion take precedence over business and pleasure, daily life and domestic concerns. Go there and you will not be disappointed, if you see it with the right eyes.

If there is time, a visit to Lucca is well worthwhile. The house where Puccini was born is open to the public and the private rooms are fascinating . to visit.

When the composer left for Paris in early April 1898 it was to arrange for the première of *La Bohème* at the Opera Comique. But the premiere was postponed, forcing Puccini to spend more than two and a half months away from home.

Ill at ease with the French language he showed little interest in the city or in the hectic social life he was forced to lead. "I came into this world to be born in and live in Torre," he wrote to Ferrucio Pagni. "I cry out — as the snow does for the sun, as coffee does for sugar — for the peace of the mountains, the valleys, the greenery, and red sunset." Poetically, he summed up his feelings in a letter written to Alfredo Caselli one month after his arrival in the French capital:-

"I am fed up with Paris. I yearn for the scented woods, with their fragrance, the undulation of my paunch within loose trousers, without a vest. I yearn for the free and fragrant wind that reaches me from the sea. I savour its salty air with dilated nostrils and wide-open lungs.

I hate pavements.

I hate large buildings.

I hate capitals.

I hate columns.

I love the beautiful columns of the poplar and the fir; the arches of shaded avenues, there to create my temple, my home, my studio. I love the green expanse of the cool shelter of the woods — old and young. I love the blackbird, the blackcap, the woodpecker. I hate the horse, the cat, the tamed sparrow, the house dog. I hate the steamer, the top hat, the tails…"

When he wrote this, the composer was not happy with the rehearsals, which were more careful than usual because of the various cast changes which had made the postponements necessary. What upset him was the enormous publicity campaign which entailed his attendance at endless receptions where he was introduced to the tout Paris which bored him and made him increasingly nervous.

By the spring of 1898 he was more than ready to devote full time to a new opera, particularly after the long period of creative inactivity in Paris. To do so, he felt that he needed to find a temporary home away from both Milan and Torre del Lago. Torre del Lago in addition to its oppressive summer heat, was too filled with friends and the temptations of hunting. To recreate the dark, brooding atmosphere of *Tosca*, he felt the need for total isolation.

"I will," he wrote to Illica, "seclude myself in a Lucchese villa, where I will at last rest my forearm on the toscano table."

The villa in which Puccini worked that summer belonged to his friend, the Marchese Raffaello Mansi. It was located in the small village of Monsagrati, one of the many tiny villages that dot the hills surrounding Lucca. A stone placed on the side of the Villa Mansi proclaims that it was there that the composer wrote the first act of *Tosca*, it does not state that it was, in effect, a kind of prison for the composer, Elvira and Fosca. All three hated it, but at least Puccini had his work to keep him occupied, while his family had nothing to fill the long gloomy days. The villa was large and comfortable, but the surroundings were ugly and oppressive. The days were blisteringly hot, so hot that the composer was forced to work at night — usually from ten o'clock till four in the morning.

Shut in among the woods, between the mountains, there was nothing to do but work; few human beings came near the place. Nonetheless, it was just that he wanted, and he planned to stay there until October! That was if he could last and if Elvira and Fosca could sustain their martyrdom and remain there for that length of time.

In spite of personal discomfort, the summer had been a productive one, and Puccini almost maintained his promise to remain in the mountain retreat until October, not leaving there until September 22. When he left — for Torre del Lago, where he could ease the burden of work with the pleasures of hunting — he was well satisfied with the progress he had made.

The composer was able to stay in Torre until the end of the year, and as always it provided him with the breathing space he badly needed. He began working on the second act, and this was, according to notes on the score, completed on July 16th. On September 29th, the third and final act of *Tosca* was completed.

Relieved that his work had come to an end and confident of its success, Puccini sent the score off to Ricordi. There was no way he could have anticipated the violent response from his publisher and friend; he disliked the opera and said the third act of *Tosca*, as it stood, "seems to me a serious error of conception and execution". Puccini was stunned by this severe if affectionate rebuke from his publisher.

However he next composed *Madam Butterfly* and became a truly international star. Most of this opera was written at his piano at Torre del Lago.

CHAPTER FIFTEEN

BROADWAY — WORKING FOR YUL BRYNNER

Like most drama students in London, you look forward towards finding a job eventually in the West End, or at least in the London area. You may be a brilliant actor but no agent is going to see you if you are playing in the wilds of Scotland or in a theatre a hundred miles from London. When my husband and I moved to Canada, purely for financial reasons, it was always with the thought that I would one day return to the theatre in London, and pick up my career there. Working in Toronto in CBC television drama and summer stock, the theatre scene was focused on what was happening in New York, not London. As soon as we could afford to, we began going to New York for weekends and seeing as many plays as possible.

On one visit, just out of curiosity, I answered a casting call advertised in *Backstage*, the trade paper in Manhattan, at the Actors' Equity offices on West 26th Street. I joined a line up at 8.30 am outside the building, standing in sub zero-temperatures, waiting to sign up on the audition lists posted inside, once the doors opened. Some actors had got up at five am to join the queue and there was still no guarantee that there would be any space left for all to audition. The whole experience was extremely depressing. I waited four hours in the lounge there, and the lists were endless. Come back tomorrow and try again! Most of the auditions were for road shows and out-of-town theatres. For Broadway you needed a good agent, a good P R person and personal manager.

That winter in Toronto was one of the coldest on record. Dark, black days when nothing seemed to be worth living for. It was the closest I ever came to thoughts of ending it all. London was out of the question, New York was impossible; I submerged myself in a daily chore of domestic duties and hopelessness. No one seemed slightly interested in the theatre at that time; there wasn't any in Toronto, only the Stratford Theatre season in the summer. I'd read about what was happening in New York when the new season started; it all seemed so impossibly difficult to make any kind of career at all.

One day I answered an advertisement in the *New York Times* for a personal assistant to assist a well-known celebrity. I mailed off my résumé and forgot all about it. A few weeks later, the phone rang and I was asked to attend an interview for the job advertised. The girl on the phone wouldn't give me the name of the celebrity so out of curiosity I went to see her. We discussed the job and my suitability; then she said that the celebrity was Yul Brynner, who was about to arrive in Toronto for a run of *The King and I*.

One week later I flew to New York to meet with Yul Brynner at the Pierre Hotel. I got the job. I was to start when the tour reached Toronto. As I flew back to Canada I realised I was about to enter the world of a "superstar", in a rarefied world of limousines, security guards, paparazzi, orchids delivered daily, Trump Tower accommodations and celebrity-studded evenings. I was back in the theatre, but not on stage. It didn't matter, at least I was in the business again. I met more celebrated actors while working for Mr. B than I could have imagined. Like Noel Coward, he knew everybody and everybody knew him. He had had a long career in Hollywood as well as on Broadway; Coward describes a meal they had together in a Chicago hotel when Yul was still in make-up as the King of Siam.

The day came when I had my first meeting with Mr B; I received a list of instructions. His former assistant was to stay on for two weeks to train me in the job. On my first day he gave me seven pages of instructions on what to do when Mr B (we always called him that, only close family called him Yul) moved from city to city on tour. Because he would be spending months on the road, he wanted each hotel suite to be his home away from home. He had already been diagnosed with lung cancer and had also an injured back, so he wanted the comforts of home. He therefore had his own double bed, his electric sun bed, his TV and video equipment, his photographic equipment and tapes all taken with him, as well as some other pieces of furniture. Thus it was necessary to have all the hotel furniture removed from the suite by the time he arrived, and his own installed. My passionate pilgrimage had begun across the States ending up on Broadway. I would be part of a scene which I had only read about, opening nights at Sardi's, invitations to important parties, friendships with theatre personalities and best of all, being in the theatre each night.

After Toronto we flew to Boston and the outgoing assistant showed me the ropes during the run there. She introduced me to his dresser, the company manager, the publicist, his agent, his lawyer and the producer of the show, Mitch Leigh.

The routine each day was the same. An hour before the show, we would sit in his dressing room while he was putting on his make-up and go through all the media requests, mail, invitations and his various requests. I was completely floored when I walked in the first night, to find him seated there, a few inches from me, his naked body clothed only in a G-string. He hated applying body make-up, so that is why he had his sun bed installed in his hotel suite.

During the tour he appeared with Mike Wallace on the TV programme *Sixty Minutes* when he announced that his cancer had gone into remission, and that because of his doctor's prescriptions he was on the way to being cured. Suddenly I was deluged with over five hundred letters a week from cancer patients begging for his advice, his doctor's phone number and address, and for the names of his medications. I started reading each and every letter; they came from all over the world — one particularly moving one from a girl in Northern Australia — and when I would take one or two of the most heartbreaking of them to him, he would say, "Tell them I can't do anything for them, I'm not a doctor." So it was tremendously difficult to answer their pleas for help. One thing he had great faith in, as far as his diet was concerned, was eating large quantities of raw carrots. Immediately he arrive at a new hotel, he would have his cook make up a large jug of carrot juice.

The tour continued. Each city was a challenge. About two weeks ahead of the tour, I would search for accommodation for him. It either had to be the Presidential Suite at a leading hotel or a luxury penthouse apartment. He preferred an hotel because of room service and the added security, as well as his own staff. Security guards had to be hired, two guards for the stage door, a guard outside his dressing room and one outside his hotel suite when he was in residence.

Two moving vans drove up on the night of the closing; next day they would take his furniture and belongings on to the next city. He had several dozen pairs of black suits, all identical, several dozen pairs of black shoes, sports equipment, and of course the entire wardrobe of Mrs B. His dressing room at each theatre had to be freshly painted in dark brown — it covered the dirt he said — and there had to be a well-stocked kitchen and refrigerator in every hotel suite on his arrival. It took a tremendous amount of organisation. His driver and limousine would take him to the airport and then would drive to the next city, where we were on hand, making sure that we picked up all his shopping requirements on the way. His driver was devoted to him and we used to spend some anxious hours waiting for Mr B's plane to arrive at the various cities. I remember in one city, the flight was delayed, and as we were both starving, we pulled into a MacDonalds and drove up to the window in the stretch limousine, ordered our two hamburgers and ate them in the limo in the parking lot, amidst the stares of the other motorists. I would meet him with a wheel chair, and he would be first off the plane with the front row seats in the

First Class section being reserved for him. I'd wheel him directly to the car and then go back for the forty pieces of luggage at the baggage claim and follow up in another car behind.

There was a checklist I would have to go through before meeting him. Were there black-out curtains in his hotel bedroom? Were there groceries, carrots in the fridge? Were there cards beside the phones with all the cast phone numbers? Was there an extra phone line installed for his private use? Was there an extra power outlet for his sun bed, as he would be using all the others for his video, TV and exercise bike? Was there the latest copy of *Variety* on the coffee table? Did I have the address of the nearest Barclays' Bank. The usual things.

Then a few weeks before Christmas we arrived in New York. The show opened at the Broadway Theatre in a snow storm but all the critics turned up and the audiences lined up around the block to get in. Mr B arranged to have a coffee urn set up outside and people standing in line were given free cups of coffee; the same was also provided for the lines of people buying tickets in the weeks to come. After working for so long on tour, it was bliss to have a settled existence. His lawyer asked me to find him a very special apartment for his return to Manhattan. I searched high and low for the right place. The spacious Park Avenue apartments either weren't near enough to the theatre or they wouldn't allow dogs. He had a dog who travelled everywhere with him. Finally just a week before the company was to arrive in New York, I found a penthouse in the Trump Tower. It didn't matter that it cost $10,000 a month in rent; his lawyer told me it had to be the best!

It was a hectic week, rearranging the furniture in readiness for his own effects and making room for the extra furniture to be brought in. The day before they arrived, Mrs B phoned me and asked me to have a large Christmas tree delivered and decorated for their arrival next day. No florists would handle such an order. "Go down to the market," they said... But no taxi would take a large Christmas tree; "Get a truck," they said. Fortunately I knew a friend who owned a truck, and he took time off work to help me buy the tree and deliver it. For the next few hours, we stocked the refrigerator, cleaned up, decorated the tree, went to the airport to meet the Brynners, collected their luggage in a second car and saw that they were well settled in. I arrived back in my apartment at midnight only to have the phone ring thirty minutes later, and Mrs B saying, "Please replace the light bulbs on the Christmas tree," because she didn't want them blinking on and off. I tried to explain that if she took the bulb out nearest the electrical plug they would stop blinking, but it was necessary for me to go over and show her how to do it.

You had to try to anticipate their every need before they asked, however this time I had failed. We were now in New York, on Broadway, and life started to accelerate.

Going to the theatre each night was always a thrill. I'd arrive early, check the mail, and then walk from the stage door through towards Mr B's dressing room. On the way, I'd walk out across the vast stage, stand centre stage and look out across the auditorium. I'd stand in the spot where Mr B would stand every night receiving a standing ovation. It always worked. He would kneel down or bow very low, and then suddenly look up, raise his arms, walk forward and the entire audience would stand. It happened every night. He brought the house down with his final curtain call, the cheering crowd most often with tears in their eyes, as everyone knew that he was fighting cancer…It took great courage for his wife to act with him on stage during the death scene at the end of the show, and towards the end of the run, when we all knew he was dying it was incredible to witness the love and affection the whole company had for him.

He was a true professional and a legend. The part of the King of Siam became his alone, and he did in fact, become the King of Broadway during that last run in New York.

He would take his curtain calls often in severe pain but then go on for dinner or to a night-club with his new young wife. The opening night on Broadway was memorable. He was incredibly brave, he survived the waltz number, *Shall We Dance*, with Anna holding him up in her arms. Later the limousine took us up to the opening night party at his son's Hard Rock Cafe on 57th Street.

After several months, the show was cancelled as Mr B was hospitalised and died shortly afterwards. Only his close family were there during the final few weeks. However one phrase has stayed with me ever since I worked with him. During his interview with Mike Wallace on the *Sixty Minutes* programme, he said he had this philosophy, and he quoted: "You are born alone, you live your life alone, and you die alone. Anyone who helps you as you journey through life you must be thankful for and be grateful."

CHAPTER SIXTEEN

PALM BEACH, FLORIDA

The following year I met a former Broadway actress who dropped her career in order to have a family; she had a house in Palm Beach, Florida. Mutual friends had introduced us and we played tennis together several times. She invited me to stay with her in Palm Beach and a great friendship began.

Returning to Coward's life, I read that he had stayed in Palm Beach and had socialised with the more prominent residents. There he goes again, I thought, amazed at his knack of knowing the right people. Do British actors or playwrights still manage to sweep into Palm Beach (if they want or need to), stopping beforehand in New York to buy some silk pyjamas and a polka-dot dressing-gown, then be taken to a glamorous reception in an exclusive mansion on the beach? You have to keep rationalising madly to keep your perspective.

The chief mover and shaker when I arrived there was Allen Manning, President of the English-Speaking Union and also of The Pundits, a men's group who meet every week and invite international guest speakers for lunch. He knew my hostess and invited us to several wonderful soirees. Some of the homes were spectacular, costing over three or four million dollars and the architecture was a mixture of Spanish and Mexican.

Mizner was a famous architect who worked in Florida and his influence is everywhere.

A drive along Ocean Boulevard reveals many homes belonging to famous people. Opposite the Bath and Tennis club is Mar-a-Lago, originally built for Mrs Merriweather Post, now owned by Donald Trump; further along is a house owned by John Lennon's widow.

This was the first time I had mixed with super-rich people who probably could have produced and promoted a play at a snap of their fingers; however I was too inhibited and unnerved to mention what I did, and nobody asked. As someone's house guest, as I was, you are barely admitted into the conversation, let alone made the subject of their attention or curiosity at a reception.

For once, my luck had turned. It was absolute luck, suddenly being introduced to the right people. I'd missed out in London, it seemed, by working only with theatre people, whereas in Palm Beach

"Society" was the phenomenon. You had to be "in" to get into those mansions.

I remember on a charter holiday to Fort Lauderdale years ago hiring a car to drive up to see Palm Beach and Worth Avenue. Driving along the Ocean Boulevard was similar to driving along the Côte d'Azur — it was more enjoyable if you saw someone who lived behind one of those pairs of enormous wrought iron gates.

First, in Palm Beach are the two private clubs, The Everglades club with a ten-year waiting list and a fifty thousand dollar initiation fee, and the Bath and Tennis club, almost as exclusive. Guests are allowed in about six times a season. There are balls, dinners and cocktail parties night after night with drinks beforehand at somebody's beach-side mansion. It is something to experience once in a lifetime. Nowhere else is there such a combination of wealth, glorious hot sun, blue ocean, white beaches, green-lit swimming-pools, liveried staff and glamorous wardrobes.

In several BBC programmes and British newspaper articles, Palm Beach residents were ridiculed, the residents, including wealthy widows and society matrons with blue rinses, were portrayed as plastic people with too much money and too much time on their hands. But the BBC or the newspapers didn't mention the fact that these people spend most of their days raising money for charity. The huge social events are all for charities. The Red Cross Ball is the biggest social event of the year. Society pages are endless, but they are mostly about charity events.

Coward met many colourful people while he was there, and after my own failure to connect with an interesting group in London, I was amazed at the cross-section I met by chance within a few weeks.

Among them was a former French teacher who had written five books on Guy de Maupassant, collected paintings by famous French novelists, and had sold his two collections of rare antique books, which enables him to move from a small house on the university campus to a magnificent art-filled apartment overlooking the ocean. He is a rare combination, an intellectual with a bawdy sense of humour. His quiz on the sexual subtitles of Shakespeare's plays extraordinary and raucous. I admired a water-colour he possessed which was painted by George Sand and another created by Flaubert.

Worth Avenue is in the centre of Palm Beach; half-way down the street there are several picturesque alley-ways leading to tiny boutiques and cafes. In one of them I met another rare personality.

Jack Owen, a Brit, who for some time had his own PR agency, wrote a book about Palm Beach scandals. As Paris has the Shakespeare and Co bookshop, where English writers meet and discuss their work over coffee, so Jack Owen has his bookshop just down the road in Lake Worth. He collects out-of-print books and does searches for customers from all over the States. He buys books at auctions and from some collections of the old families in Palm Beach. His bookshop is a gathering-place for writers and each year he organises readings of local poets and other writers.

Then there is another British expatriate, a fanatic of George Bernard Shaw and Beethoven. He is the Serendipity Editor for the big, glossy society magazine, and is also their restaurant critic as well. Reviewing the restaurants in Palm Beach must be one of the joys of the job. He took me to Renato's, a celebrated eating spot off Worth Avenue, to review the chef. The meal was delectable, and so was the company. I regularly send him A A Gill's reviews from *The Sunday Times* and the two of them surely must meet.

Then there was Laurence Learner, another good tennis partner who had just finished his book on the Kennedys, and Caroline Whittey, the charming blonde Real Estate agent, who negotiated the sale of multi-million homes and held parties in them. She also helped set up the first International Piano Competition held every year.

There was another interesting resident who was a collector, not of antique books, but more unusually, of antique car badges, the plaques you used to see on the bumpers of Jaguars and Rolls Royces, before they became to valuable to be left on the exterior of the cars. He must own about four hundred of them, and he travels the world finding, buying and trading them.

Last but not least are a couple who give the largest and most marvellous party at Christmas time. Carmen and Bill Bissell have a home in Shelter Island, just north of Long Island, and one in West Palm Beach. They throw their parties by the swimming-pool which is surrounded by palm trees. She invites poets, painters, writers, actors, bankers and indeed everybody who is interesting, and you tend to meet more artistic people there than at all the other events during the year. Carmen is also an accomplished painter; her house is full of her work, as well as that of other artists; two of my works hang in her Shelter Island home. She always introduces me as the woman from Tasmania. The atmosphere is full of Christmas spirit, laughter and talk.

Many people who visit the area wonder why people enjoy it when there is so much more going on in Miami, but it is a much quieter spot. Sooner or later you can't help thinking of the gloom and doom of London weather, so it is wretched when you have to return via Heathrow and plunge into the vast sea of the drizzling rain.

CHAPTER SEVENTEEN

GEORGE SAND'S CHATEAU IN FRANCE

Chateau de Nohant (George Sand and Chopin)

"If music be the food of love play on..."

During my stay in Palm Beach, I met an Australian pianist, Alan Kogosowski, who gave a Chopin recital at the magnificent Flagler Museum. He specialises in Chopin's music and has just completed composing a third movement to Chopin's unfinished *Third Piano Concerto*. His playing was brilliant and after hearing him play several more times I truly believed he deserves world recognition which he will surely receive before long.

He revived a lifelong dream I had which was to visit the French chateau where Chopin lived with the writer George Sand while he was composing much of his music. To me Chopin represented love, pure undissembling love. Both my husband and I had struggled through learning some of his better known works. Although I can still play the *Military Polonaise* and some of the *Etudes*, hearing Alan play made me realise what a genius he is. Even though he was a pupil of Malcuzynski, he has his own unique individual style. He had been giving a series of concerts at Sotheby's in London for several years. His playing confirmed my resolution to visit the Chateau de Nohant.

For years, ever since I started practising the piano, I had tried to visualise what the house looked like. It dates me to say I saw the film, *Song to Remember*, starring Cornel Wilde and Merle Oberon, but the film left an indelible passion in me to learn first of all as much of Chopin's music as possible, and also one day visit Nohant.

The Chateau de Nohant is a three hour drive from Paris, down over the Loire to Chateauroux and on to La Châtre.

A few months later, we were on our way there at last! The expectancy was wonderful. I had waited for years to be where we were now, driving along a French country road on the way to Nohant. In an hour or so I would see Chopin's piano, his room, her room and where the two of them had worked together for many years. It couldn't have been at a better time of year, high summer, and there were fields of sunflowers on either side of the road.

99

We spent the last hour twisting and turning up and down roads outside La Châtre trying to come across the house. It was tantalising and finally I spotted the sign ahead, CHATEAU DE NOHANT. We turned down a short driveway and there it was, a lovely old manor house with large wrought iron gates and a small gate-house.

George Sand's grandmother bought Nohant and settled there. When Aurore (George Sand) was still a child her mother brought her to Nohant and received a large settlement for her daughter by giving her up to Aurore's grandmother and forfeiting the right to bring up the young Aurore at Nohant. So this was her home from her earliest years.

She learnt to ride, to live as a country hostess and her grandmother instilled in her all the Parisian manners that she too had been taught. When she met Chopin she had already found her place in Parisian society and could introduce him to the leading figures in the world of Arts and Music in the city. She had fled an unfortunate marriage and left her husband in charge of Nohant. She had to support herself, and therefore started writing, first with co-authors, of whom Alfred de Musset was one, and then later by her own hand. Her husband drank and spent all the estate income from Nohant so finally she managed to pay him off and get rid of him. However she then had to return to Nohant each year to oversee the farm and income from it.

When she met Chopin she was already well-known as a novelist and playwright. At one time she had four plays running simultaneously in Paris. Contributing factors to the final break-up with Chopin were her daughter and son. Solange, her daughter, tried to persuade Chopin to side with her when she wanted to marry a man who Sand disliked, and Maurice her son was jealous of Chopin's place in his mother's affections. They all spent a great deal of their time at Nohant and there are many different reports of what happened when Chopin came to stay there.

Anyone who admires the delicacy of Chopin's music must find it hard to believe that he could compose such music in a house which was not only freezing cold at most times of the year, but also full of domestic quarrelling.

In 1830, Marie d'Agoult arrived at Nohant with a portrait of her lover, Franz Liszt. Sand put her up in the downstairs bedroom and moved upstairs to the end bedroom. She redecorated her room with blue and white wallpaper which visitors can admire to this day.

Shortly afterwards, Liszt arrived, and it was then that a stream of celebrities started visiting the house. You can still see her dinner service and glassware set up on the dining room table, together with the place-names of her dinner guests who included Gustave Flaubert, Turgeniev

100

and Balzac. While Balzac was staying with her, he was introduced to the comforting pleasure of opium. He later wrote in his *Traite des Excitants Modernes*, "I owe the key to this treasure to George Sand."

He wrote in a rather unkind long letter to a friend, that having reached Nohant around seven-thirty in the evening he had found George Sand, "in her dressing-gown, smoking an after-dinner cigar by the fire in a huge, empty room. She was wearing a pretty pair of yellow, fringed slippers, coquettish stockings, and red trousers…Physically, she had developed a double chin, like a Church canon. She hasn't a single white hair, notwithstanding her dreadful misfortunes. Her dark complexion hasn't changed; her lovely eyes are as lustrous as ever. She still looks stupid when sunk in thought, for, as I told her after studying her for a while, her expression is concentrated in her eyes. She has been at Nohant for the past year, very despondent and working her head off. She leads much the same life as I do. She goes to bed at six in the morning and gets up at noon; I go to bed at six in the evening and get up at midnight. but naturally I conformed myself to her habits, and for three days we talked from five in the evening…until five in the morning, with the result that I learned more about her, and *vice verse*, in those three long conversations than in the four preceding years, when she loved Sandeau and was involved with Musset…"

The manor house consists of two floors. As you come in the front door there is an elegant foyer and a sweeping circular staircase up to the first floor. On the ground floor you pass directly into the main salon which contains the dining table and chairs in the centre on the room, Above it is a Venetian chandelier which Sand probably brought back from one of her stays in Venice. French windows open out to a flight of steps to the garden. To the right of this room is a second salon with the piano, family portraits and some of her original furniture. To the left is a main bedroom and the study where Sand did her writing. She used to write through the night and after her children were born, she said it was the only time she found enough peace to be able to work.

Turning the corner in the hall you enter into a small theatre. This is where Sand entertained her house guests with her new plays. The stage is still set with props and furniture that was used for one of her plays. She and Chopin used to take part in some of these productions. On the right wall of the theatre is a small puppet stage where she would write special plays for her son Maurice. In a glass case nearby there are dozens of beautifully dressed puppets, most of the clothes being made by Sand herself. There are caricatures of village people she knew and hosts of other recognisable people.

Walking up the staircase to the second floor you can almost hear the voices and music of the people who lived here. Upstairs the bedrooms are all facing the garden with a corridor along the length of the house, but with inter-connecting doors to each room. Sand's son Maurice, an artist, had his studio in the attic. There is still some original furniture left in Sand's bedroom. You feel their presence and spirits are still there, however it helps to visit the Chateau when there are few tourists around, preferably late afternoon.

After viewing the house, we walked through the gardens and found the tiny walled cemetery nearby in the grounds. Here we observed George Sand's grave together with that of her son Maurice and other family members. The gardens are very extensive and lead into a small tree-filled park with covered walks and benches where Chopin must have walked for hours. The only sound heard were bird calls and the wind in the overhanging trees. I had taken a portable CD player with some Chopin music and fortunately there were no other visitors, so we sat in the garden for quite some time listening to some of the music that we knew from research had been composed there.

One of my other passionate pilgrimages was to visit the monastery in Majorca where Sand and Chopin lived for one winter. He composed on an upright piano in a small stone cell — both still exist. He wrote to a friend in Paris:

"I am in Palma, among the palms, cedars, cacti, olive trees, pomegranates etc, everything the Jardin des Plantes has in its greenhouses. A sky like turquoise, a sea like lapis lazuli, mountains like emeralds, air like heaven. Sun all day; everyone in summer clothing; at night guitars and singing for hours. Huge balconies with grapevines, overhead; Moorish walls. Everything looks towards Africa, as the town does. In a word, a glorious life!"

But it was not to last. The weather changed and both of them became ill. Sand wrote that she thought Chopin might die. He was deathly ill, and they journeyed to Nohant just in time.

Each year in July there is a festival of music at Nohant. Famous pianists come to play at the Chateau and the concerts take place in the old barn nearby. Information can be obtained from the French Tourist Board or the Syndicat d'Initiative at La Châtre, the nearest town. Reservations are advised.

CHAPTER EIGHTEEN

BACK TO THE THEATRE

After the death of my parents in Tasmania —they are buried together in a country churchyard in Campbell Town — I wanted to live where we spent our happiest time together. Although Hobart is one of the most picturesque, romantic, cleanest places in the world, it is very remote, far away from the West End, so the second choice was London. I still mourn them, so, as we had been together for a few months when I was a student in the UK, I chose London. I found a flat in Covent Garden and looked for work.

I had been away so long I had lost touch with my friends; Harold Innocent, the actor, was the only person I'd kept in contact with. We were in Rep together years ago in Felixstowe. I was shocked and saddened by his death a few years ago.

Walking up Charing Cross Road, I remembered knocking on agents' doors and doing the rounds. Even in those early days I wondered why do we do it. Watching the world disasters on television, why not join the Red Cross, become a missionary, do voluntary work, something intelligent? I remember once in desperation, going into a hospital and asking if I could help. They thought I was mad. I was brimming with despair. Could I read to the children, perhaps, or hold someone's hand? Looking for work as an actor seemed insane. The rudeness, the rejections, the waiting is well known, but how much of it could you take? Do actors really matter? Do any actors influence people's lives by their performance beyond breakfast the next day? How can you say "Get a Life" to an out-of-work actor — when he gladly would if he could!

Then I found the following extract written by Hazlitt:

"Players are 'the abstracts and brief chronicles of the time'; the motley representatives of human nature. They are the only hypocrites. Their life is a dream; a studied madness. The height of their ambition is to be beside themselves. Today kings, tomorrow beggars, it is only when they are themselves, that they are nothing.

"Made up of mimic laughter and tears, passing from the extremes of joy or woe at the prompter's call, they wear the livery of other men's fortunes; their very thoughts are not their own.

"They are, as it were, train bearers in the pageant of life,

103

and hold a glass up to humanity, frailer than itself. We see ourselves at second hand in them: they show us all that we are, all that we wish to be, and all that we dread to be.

"They teach us when to laugh and when to weep, when to love and when to hate upon principle and with a good grace! Wherever there is a playhouse, the world will go on.

"The stage not only refines the manners, but it is the best teacher of morals, for it is the truest and most intelligible picture of life."

It glances a mortifying reflection on the shortness of human life, and the vanity of human pleasures. Something reminds us, that "all the world's a stage, and all the men and women merely players."

For the past six years, I've been running a showcase for young actors and actresses in the West End. I've tried to give over two hundred performers a chance to be seen. Vincent Shaw is one of the agents who has come to see their work, and he has given hope to many of them. He has spent his life in the theatre and of course helped Jessie Matthews to stardom. I've always asked performers to dress formally for these showcases.

Some people criticise Sir Noel and his plays but his advice to actors is legendary. He really did believe that dress and manners in the theatre, either back stage or on front, were supremely important. He wrote that if he was going to play a dustman, he would have his suit pressed for rehearsals, out of respect for the theatre itself, the edifice, the building. And on theatre: "It can be vulgar, but it must never be embarrassing."

Dear Noel, how we miss you
Dear Noel how we grieve
There will never be anyone like you
We know that —let's not be deceived.

You travelled the world when writing your plays
You captured nations! — and started a craze —
The dressing gowns, the parties, "destiny's tot"
A "Coward" sort of person was tremendously "hot" !

The laughter, the wit on the tip of your tongue
Made us all feel glamorous and kept us so young
You strove to teach us manners —
And above all, to have fun.
No dismal kitchen sink dramas
To you, it was "not done".

Actors and actresses were kept in their place
If they started to mumble, it was such a disgrace.

The Riviera, the Bahamas…those exotic sights,
Prompted you to play writing and brilliant first nights.

"Heigh Ho" were the words you used when times were tough
"Heigh Ho"…was all when you were down on your luck
But never for long, there was always work to be done
Rise above it, get on with it, Life goes on…
Forget the critics, banish the blues
Never be defeated…stuff the reviews.

You pricked the balloon of pretentious new writers
You couldn't stand filth or long pregnant pauses.
Relative Values says it all so clearly
"We are what we come from," and Maugham agreed entirely.
Your motto in life if problems arose
Was to *Sail Away* on some ship
Till you buried your woes.

On the pavements of Paris during the war
Noel Coward trod lightly, he was no bore.
To criticise Nazis when they showed such defence
To think they could conquer the whole sordid mess.

He took an apartment in the Place Vendome
He held court there as if it were home.

The fact was…that Noel was hooked
And he wrote to Head Office that he was staying for good.

But alas they beckoned him home without much ado.
Back to London, to tell Whitehall, who was who.

Later on, much later after the war
Noel decided if he were to do it at all
He'd better go back there and play something in French
And Voila! He did so, in his own play no less.

Because of the taxman, we waved you Goodbye
We missed you in England, but then you were building Firefly!
Your canvases full of wonderful colours,
We knew you were not living with a group of old dullards
Ian Fleming, Errol Flynn, not to mention Graham and Cole,
They knew you were writing all those memorable roles.

Dear Noel we must thank you for all that you've done
To bring such happiness to this world so wrung.
Now that you're gone...who knows where?
Perhaps Shakespeare is listening to your wit, so rare.

The crowds should always dress, perfumed and showered
When they attend a first night, of a play by Noel Coward!

Addresses

The Actors' Centre — 1A Tower Street Covent Garden

The Grill Room, Cafe Royal — Regent Street, near Piccadilly Circus

The Caprice Restaurant — Arlington Street, off Piccadilly near The Ritz

Coliseum Theatre — St Martin's Lane, Covent Garden

The Concert Artists' Club — 20 Bedford Street

Noel Coward's house — 17 Gerald Road, Pimlico

David Drummond's Theatre Book Shop — Cecil Court, off St Martin's Lane

Charles Dickens' home — Doughty Street, off Theobald's Road

Dress Circle Shop — 37 Monmouth Street, near Seven Dials

French's Theatre Bookshop — Fitzroy St, Fitzrovia

The Garrick Club — 15 Garrick Street, Covent Garden

David Garrick's house — 25 Southampton Street, Covent Garden

The Globe Theatre, New Globe Walk— SE1 near London Bridge

Half-price ticket booth — south side of Leicester Square

Ivy Restaurant — West Street, opposite the Ambassador Theatre

Kettners Restaurant — behind Cambridge Circus

The Lamb and Flag — Rose Court, off Garrick Street

The National Portrait Gallery — next to Trafalgar Square

Ivor Novello's flat — 11 The Aldwych (off the Strand)

The Old Vic Theatre — Waterloo Road, near Waterloo Station

107

Palace Theatre — Cambridge Circus

The Players Club — Villiers St, (next to Charing Cross Station)

The Playhouse Theatre — Northumberland Avenue

The Royal Opera House — Bow Street (renovations 1997-1999)

Rules Restaurant — 35 Maiden Lane, Covent Garden

Savoy Theatre — off the Strand

Bernard Shaw's home — 29 Fitzroy Square, Fitzrovia

St Paul's Church — opposite 20 Bedford Street

Sir Arthur Sullivan's statue — Embankment Gardens, behind the Savoy

The Theatre Museum — Russell Street, at Bow Street, Covent Garden

The Theatre Royal — Catherine Street, Covent Garden (*not Drury Lane*)

Virginia Woolf's home — 37 Mecklenburgh Square, then 38 Brunswick Square

PLAYS BY ELIZABETH SHARLAND

The Private Life of George Bernard Shaw, Theatre Museum, London
The Last Weekend, A T A, New York
Paths of Escape, A T A, New York
To Kill a Critic, A T A, New York
The Wardrobe Mistress, King's Head Theatre, London
It's Too Late, King's Head Theatre, London
Beyond the Footlights
Quite By Accident
Jamaican Interlude
Love from Shakespeare to Coward (Anthology), Theatre Museum, London
Noel Coward and Friends, Concert Artists' Association, London
Liszt in Love, Concert Artists' Association, London